UP A NOTCH

TAG Publishing, LLC
2030 S. Milam
Amarillo, TX 79109
www.TAGPublishers.com
Office (806) 373-0114
Fax (806) 373-4004
info@TAGPublishers.com

ISBN:978-1-59930-425-0

First Edition

Quantity discounts are available on bulk orders.
Contact info@TAGPublishers.com for more information.

UP
A
NOTCH

Oliver C. Pecora

CONTENTS

DEDICATION

This book is dedicated to those people whom have crossed my path through my journey of life thus far - to those who have believed in me and who saw me bigger than I saw myself.

A special thanks to my wife, Lea. She has stood by me through so many lessons learned. She also helped during the editing process of this book, which was made better by her efforts. I love and appreciate her more than she knows.

INTRODUCTION

Becoming an entrepreneur who perseveres with passion is within your reach. Also within your reach is the ability to create a truly fulfilling life, one with enough time and money to do the things you really want to do. Building a business is a tool to help achieve this often sought out objective. Thus, a business needs to be profitable and fulfilling for the entrepreneur, the manager and the staff. Achieving this takes vision, strategy, focus, communication, commitment and time: *Vision* to what specific purpose the organization serves; *Strategy* through preparation, planning and systems; *Focus* through care and disciplined action; *Communication* through leadership; *Commitment* through dedicated people; *Time* through patience and perseverance.

In this book we will discuss the benefits of enhanced awareness in the role of a leader as well as the positive impact it has on an organization. We will also discuss the significance of human relationships in our personal and professional lives – as well as how they relate to the well-being of not only the organization you are trying to build, but the people that make it possible. An organization armed properly can not only survive, but thrive - even in the most challenging economic times.

In this book we will discuss the challenge, the journey, the thought process, the solution and finally the reward. You will know that you are not alone and that we can learn from each other.

For me it all started by reaching for what I often call "The American Dream." Returning to the United States in 1997 I wanted to take owning my own business to the next level. Having spent the 10 previous years abroad in my native country, Germany, acquiring a degree in mechanical engineering, as well as co-founding a consulting company from which I gained valuable experience – I was ready to set sail back to the United States.

Born in Frankfurt, Germany and moving back and forth between the United States and Europe while growing up, I have had the opportunity to develop a broader view of the world, having been embedded in different cultures. I grew up in a family that owned a variety of businesses such as a delicatessen, restaurant, painting and decorating service, a machine shop and a metal stamping company. As a young man I worked in every one of the family businesses in both countries. It was during this time that I learned a variety of the disciplines that have guided me throughout the years. Working in each business also gave me a peek into different types of industries – ranging from retail locations where you're waiting for the customer to walk through the door, to a service business where you are visiting different job sites.

As an entrepreneur in the past twenty-plus years – having started several businesses – I have achieved many of my material dreams. This didn't come without failures and businesses that just didn't work out. It also didn't come without learning difficult lessons in dealing with people, be it business partners, subcontractors or employees. Last, it also didn't come without reaching sheer exhaustion and burn-out so often found in the role of an entrepreneur.

At times I questioned if it was all worth it. Taking a step back, I took a long hard look at *why I am really doing what it is that I am doing every day*. This question took me on a journey – a journey of self-analysis and enhanced awareness.

Having joined, observed and helped many of my peers over so many years go through various stages in building their businesses, as well as watching nearly *all* of my own families' businesses captivate their owners in one way or another, I vowed to find another way.

With a clearing vision, not only that of the organization but that of *me* the leader, I discovered the importance that a sense of *purpose*, as well as ongoing *passion*, plays in a leader's life and its connection to personal *fulfillment*. There is an absolute need for *balance* between work and play that has a direct effect on a desired outcome. The perspective gained by taking a step back, looking in the mirror and learning from what did and did not work, aids greatly in the realignment of a new strategy. Armed and energized, you are able to take yet another giant leap forward. That is why I called this book "*Up a Notch*".

My primary inspiration for writing this book is to share with others what I have learned. My wish is to help *ambitious* people navigate less painfully through their journey toward success than I did. I enjoy the idea of being able to help others who have a burning desire and dream to do something – whatever it is that is meaningful to them – and succeed at it. The thought of this is exciting to me and gives me energy and fulfillment at every turn.

By writing this book I am sharing these important insights and concepts that moved a once wearied and overwhelmed entrepreneur to new heights. I hope you – the reader – will gain valuable insights to align your own journey in the most efficient and gratifying manner. Be it building your own business, running one, or simply being inspired to awaken and develop your entrepreneurial side – which I believe everyone has – there are ways to bring more meaning into what you do everyday. This carries over and inspires those you lead and everyone you come into contact with, giving new *life* and meaning to an organization that will better serve you, your team, and your customers. Creating this kind of organization will lead you towards a truly fulfilling life, one with enough time and money to do the things you really want to do. Such an organization endures and is worth building.

CHAPTER ONE

Nothing But Headaches

The business world is often considered to be a tough environment, one of extreme challenges and competition. At best, it is unpredictable. Some would say "business is a jungle" or "business is dog eat dog." While going into business doesn't necessarily present any *physical* dangers, the business world is certainly one in which the strong survive and the weak are left by the wayside. Yet, even with this description, existing businesses grow and thrive, and new businesses are opened every minute of every day. Something attracts people to the world of business.

Why do people go into business? Several reasons come to mind – money, fulfillment, control. The reasons are as varied as the kinds of people who set out on their own. Although there is no one set pattern, you can group the reasons that most people go into business into one of several divisions.

This vision, or sense of mission, is what drives some entrepreneurs to create an organization. Often these organizations are not designed solely to earn a profit, but to effect a change in the world. The advice has often been given regarding business

– *Find a need, and fill it.* There is no lack of "needs" in the world, and also no lack of people who are eager to make a living and prosper by filling those needs. Sometimes that sense of mission is what sets a particular business apart from its competitors.

While a person might go into the world of business because of any number of reasons, a person becomes an entrepreneur only when certain factors are in force. By their very nature entrepreneurs are optimists and risk takers. They believe that they can succeed in creating a product or service that the world needs and will pay for. Starting your own business is a leap of faith that not everyone can take.

The entrepreneur is a gambler – not the kind who will walk up to a roulette wheel in a casino and lay all of their money on a number, but the kind who will study the cards and see if they can find an advantage which they can capitalize on. Being an entrepreneurial-style gambler doesn't mean that you leave everything completely to chance. It means that you're not afraid to take a calculated risk, while doing everything you can to create conditions that are in your favor.

Entrepreneurs are also creators. The impulse to create is part of human nature, and it is even stronger in those who are drawn to start their own business. They love the idea of realizing a dream, of building something that didn't exist before. Their mechanism may be to start a business from scratch, to buy a franchise and introduce it to a new market, or do something within an existing company. In all cases, entrepreneurs are drawn to the idea of making something that didn't exist previously.

By definition, entrepreneurs have to be visionaries. They have the ability to see a future that others don't see, a future that they believe strongly in and have the ability to create. Often they become absorbed with this vision, spending enormous amounts of time and energy working on plans to bring the vision into reality.

The entrepreneurial spirit means such people have a sense of possibility, rather than impossibility.

What this means is that entrepreneurs see deficiencies, lapses and lacks in the world as it exists. What's more, they see how they have the unique perspective to fill a need and add value to the world around them, as well as enhance the quality of their own life. Often, they may simply see an opportunity to create a product or service in an area of interest, or have experience in a field and decide to go into business for themselves. Entrepreneurs love the process of starting up something new. They envelop themselves in the construction of the organization they envision. Often, especially at the start of a new venture, entrepreneurs find themselves doing just about everything in their business on their own. After all, the entrepreneur is the only person who is committed to fulfill the vision they are setting out to achieve. It is in their mind's eye. Until this often vivid vision has taken physical form and is in sync with what they have in mind, the entrepreneur will keep on searching.

When I first started SIC Consulting after returning to the United States from Germany in 1997, I set out to build my own company.

This wasn't my first company, so I knew what I had to do and got to work. I had many people around me wondering why I wasn't seeking a "real" job. After all I had a degree in mechanical engineering.

At that time, when I first met my wife and we were dating, her parents were wondering what I was going to do with my life since they didn't see me working a regular job earning a stable income. Fortunately that didn't bother me much as I had gotten used to these types of concerns from people around me.

Unfortunately, the people that are most likely to impede your success are those closest to you.

They don't really intend any harm, but their objections are from their own frame of reference. I've heard all of the following comments at one time or another in my own life.

- *Why do that?*

- *It will never work!*

- *Who do you think you are?*

- *Get a real job.*

- *Why take on all that responsibility?*

- *It takes money to build a company.*

- *There's no security and no benefits.*

- *You're not cut out for that!*

- *It's all about luck. You have to be in the right place at the right time.*

- *Don't reach too high, you may be disappointed.*

Entrepreneurs know that they have to get as far away from that mindset as possible. Often the voices are from people they know and care about, so the objections carry more weight. However, if they listen to those protesting voices, budding entrepreneurs will lose the courage to go their own way.

The best course is to thank them for their concern and opinion. Tell them that this is the road you choose to follow. You can say something like, "I am investing my time and energy in it because it is what I want to do. It excites me, and I am confident in my abilities. Don't worry, I'll be fine." Whatever your dream is, share it. Let others feel your excitement and enthusiasm – it's infectious. Sharing your dreams and inspirations with others makes it more real – also for you. It gets you going.

You will notice that successful entrepreneurs surround themselves with people that support them in their journeys as well as challenge them to reach new heights.

It didn't take long before my new company began gaining momentum and things started to build up and I got my first handful of customers. My vision began to become real.

Besides the personal pressures, entrepreneurship can have its challenges in the world of business. It takes time, focus, commitment and a whole lot of discipline, mainly because you are running against the stream of pretty much everyone else. Entrepreneurs look for new paths to success, and others feel compelled to create obstacles.

Excitement and controlling your own destiny is one of the key attractions of being an entrepreneur. The freedom to make their own choices, and to fail or succeed because of them, is a "rush". They have the freedom to apply their own knowledge and experience to situations, and to see the outcome. Such people derive from their business decisions the same thrill that skydivers and other risk-takers seek.

The most commonly recognized attraction for those who build a business is the opportunity to prosper financially. Most fortunes are made, not inherited. In fact, in their book *The Millionaire Next Door*, authors Thomas J. Stanley and William D. Danko found that the majority of millionaires in America were small business owners who had built their businesses and their fortunes themselves. Even those who don't pursue such a path understand that owning one's own business is the surest way to wealth.

When I started SIC Consulting, which quickly evolved into a full service IT business, I had just moved back from Germany after ten years abroad. I basically just wanted to return to the United States, take what I had learned in Germany, and start over on my own. I wanted to be in control of my day and make a decent living.

My previous experience co-founding another consulting company in Germany and working with partners was good, but I liked the idea of not having to justify my time or what I was doing. Most of all I wanted to set out and create a new vision. All this spurred excitement and gave me the energy to move through the many challenges that would come at me.

Problems in Business

Even in ideal business situations, a business owner can suffer disappointments. The biggest one, of course, is the failure of the business. After having put one's heart into an endeavor, watching it fail despite your best efforts can be crushing. Regardless of the reason for the failure, seeing one's work produce less than the desired results can be heart-breaking.

Sometimes the entrepreneur can't get financing for the project. Sometimes it can be due to a tight credit climate. It may be due to the entrepreneur's credit worthiness, or just a lack of a clear vision and a financially viable business plan to attract anyone to lend money.

In a larger business, often when an employee has a great idea or wants to start a new project, corporate politics may reject the idea, or executives may want to divert funds to another project they have in mind. Very few ideas or businesses come to fruition without any money. The disappointment and frustration from not even being able to get a project off the ground is perhaps worse than seeing a new idea or perhaps the business fail. Unrealized dreams can haunt a person for a lifetime.

Disappointing also is when a business owner or entrepreneur has misread the business climate or the market. Despite the best plans, circumstances often seem to conspire against a business' success.

A person might open a small shop in the right location with the right market, when suddenly a large franchise opens next door, offering lower prices and possessing a larger advertising budget. Another may have a great idea but have underestimated the time and effort it takes to build enough demand to make ends meet.

Such a situation might have been avoidable, or it might not. Regardless, when you realize that your business has met an obstacle that may kill it, it's only natural that you should be disappointed. When the obstacle is caused by a gap in your planning, the disappointment is intensified. Each of us does the best we can but being human we sometimes make mistakes, and those mistakes lead to disappointments.

Frustration is also a constant companion for the entrepreneur or even the established and mature businessperson. Whereas disappointment is when expected results are not achieved, frustration is when progress toward a goal is slowed, more difficult or even stopped by circumstances.

The business owner's frustrations are many – everything from employee problems to problems with partners to everything in-between. Even the best-trained employees don't always perform and act as they're supposed to, and personnel problems are always a concern. Business partners are people as well, and they have all the idiosyncrasies that human beings have. A partner's non-business issues often become problems for the business.

Unexpected expenses, low cash flow, facilities or equipment that breaks down, interference from government and regulatory agencies – all of these slow or stop progress toward having a successful and profitable business. Even experienced business people suffer frustrations when an obstacle is in the way. Living with frustration is part of the package when you have your own business.

My biggest frustrations have involved managing people. Getting people to do what I wanted them to hasn't always been easy. In the early days I often handled this poorly. I just *expected* performance and efficiency. It was extremely frustrating to have a customer yell at me for something I didn't do, and then top it off by not wanting to pay for the time we had spent on a job. I spent painful moments cleaning up other people's messes and putting out fires —situations created by people I hired to do the job.

An area of extreme sensitivity for me is the sense of entitlement that my contractors or employees often had when it came to money. Money is always a sensitive subject. In the context of people you hire to do a job, a sense of entitlement on their part can easily lead to disgruntled staff that are literally working against you.

I have always worked hard to pay fairly for anyone that worked for me, and at times I have even overpaid people, trying to use money as a motivator. I have learned that money often isn't the only issue. Even when people are paid well, other issues such as jealousy seem to come up and complicate things. No amount of money will fix the problem when a strong sense of entitlement was at hand. Some people have an inflated idea of their personal value (often ego based) to the business. I've talked until I am blue in the face trying to justify to such people what it takes to keep the business going, to balance out things financially when things go wrong, etc. – something I no longer bother doing because it is ineffective.

I learned that what I said didn't matter when the person feeling a sense of entitlement believes they are doing most of the work for the client. They completely underestimate all other components that make a business work. I've even had long-term employees tell me they should get seventy-five percent of the earnings and that the rest was enough for me and all other expenses.

Of course everyone, employees, vendors and others, want to be "partners" when things are going well. Few will ever really work hard for it.

Even fewer will ever put any risk capital up, let alone put a loan against their house to finance the next investment. They all think it should come from the profits that the business generates after everyone gets paid a full paycheck. Everyone wants the benefits but not the responsibility or risk. The business owner takes on everything.

With all of the problems, every day challenges and frustrations, the entrepreneur or established business owner can begin to experience self-doubt. In time, this becomes draining and sets in motion a whole new set of events that begin to have negative effects on the business and its staff – ultimately resulting in unhappy customers and loss of business.

Add these *issues* to the many other responsibilities an entrepreneur has and even the most optimistic person is hard-pressed not to feel some doubt and become overwhelmed.

Even more treacherous is the assault on one's confidence when the project or business gets off the ground and it doesn't live up to the entrepreneur's expectations. Regardless of the cause of the failure, the entrepreneur naturally believes that he should have done a better job, either planning or in executing his plan. His natural optimism and confidence may be shaken when he discovers that he has misjudged.

Starting a new venture, either as an entrepreneur or working within a larger organization, demands extreme commitment in time, discipline and emotions. Part of the strength of the entrepreneur is his ability to focus almost completely on the project at hand. This tunnel vision allows him to avoid discouragement from the frustrations and disappointments that inevitably accompany launching a new venture.

That very strength, however, can also create a disconnect from the rest of his world. His friends, family and other relationships may suffer from a lack of attention. While a temporary imbalance is not particularly traumatic, the entrepreneur can become trapped by the very mindset that helps him create a business.

I know this to be true not only from my own experience but also in observing other business owners I have met over the years. Prior to starting my own business I actually had a life outside of the office, a life that involved motorcycle riding, skiing, and water sports. I even flew as a private pilot, enjoying cool trips such as flying over the Grand Canyon, landing on Catalina Island, circling downtown San Francisco and an occasional trip to places like Baja Mexico. I spent time with friends in beer gardens, enjoying nature, getting together for dinner, traveling, etc.

When kids came into the picture, I took on additional responsibilities. Before I knew it I found myself stuck going back and forth between the office and house. For several years I spent little time with friends and pretty much let every hobby go. With a growing family and a growing business, I didn't have much time left.

Building a business takes a lot of time and attention. Simple, mundane problems may absorb an inordinate amount of the attention. There is a continuous demand on a growing business often requiring nearly all of the entrepreneur's time. There is a lot to be said for paying attention to detail in delivering the customer a quality product. On the other hand, such a fascination with the minutiae of the business may provide little time for the problems confronting children, spouses, or friends who are in need.

When the stress of getting a business off the ground becomes too much for the entrepreneur, he may find himself making decisions that go against his beliefs and core values. Taking shortcuts, not watching finances, missing deadlines, not taking time for a break and expecting the same from employees, etc. –

sadly, these are not uncommon in stressful business situations. The entrepreneur may attempt to conceal such decisions from those closest to him, thus enlarging a gap of his own making. At the very time when he needs it most, he separates himself from his support structure.

Sometimes the entrepreneur's life gets so out of balance that he finds himself asking if his goal is worth it. He has gotten so caught up in the doing that he begins to feel disengaged with life itself. The venture, always demanding his time, leaves him little or no time for anything else – including time for those things most important.

How did this happen? It was fun when it started – the excitement of starting a new venture, putting all your time and energy into creating something. Then you find that your quality of life has suffered and you lack a connection to other people, other ways of life, or even other topics of conversation. You have become a workaholic!

When I first got out of school, I lived in Regensburg, Germany. My business was in Frankfurt, a two and a half hour trip – driving at 100-125 mph on the autobahn. I really liked my home in Regensburg. I had studied there, and had a lot of friends.

My cousin and I both worked at the business, but although I worked extremely hard during the week – sometimes until two or three in the morning – I always left Friday afternoon and spent the weekend with my friends back home.

My cousin, on the other hand, spent weekends at the business. He didn't always like that I took off every weekend. I vividly remember telling him, "You drag your feet, hang over your desk in the afternoon, and you're on the verge of burn-out. I don't believe that you're more efficient than I am when I take a break on the weekends, fully recharge, and come back to work energized and ready to go."

Several years later I was back in the United States after having started my own company – this time on my own.

One day I looked up and realized that I had fallen into the same trap that my cousin was in, and for which I had chastised him. I had people around me telling me the same thing that I had told him.

Yes, I wanted to strangle those people who were telling me to take a break – as if it were that easy. However, I eventually came to realize that I was indeed following an unproductive pattern. I broke through and started working smarter, not harder. Today I can't thank those people enough for their message to me. Where would I be today if they hadn't had the courage to tell me how it really is? They saw me as I really was - they were on the outside looking in.

Even more tragic is when the entrepreneur is successful and consciously decides that a gap exists between him and those closest to him. Giddy with success and perhaps wealth, he lets his new situation define who he is as a person. Like an uprooted tree, the entrepreneur is moved by whatever particular breeze catches him. This disconnect often results in broken relationships and discarding of those who helped him achieve his success.

What this means is that it is easy for the entrepreneur, or anyone starting a new venture, to lose his true center, and the anchors that provide him with the stability he needs in his life. Overwhelmed by problems (or success) he begins to feel as though he alone is responsible for his situation. This emotional isolation causes all sorts of problems.

The relationship issues mentioned earlier are all too common. I have personally experienced some of them and I have watched other successful business owners navigate through others. Some of the most successful people I have ever met have, at times in their life, had situations that were far from pleasant.

Also heart wrenching is when the entrepreneur loses sight of his original dream.

Each problem has become worse than the one before, he has compromised his values, his decisions have become based on expediency rather than strategy or planning – suddenly the entire project becomes different from what he originally envisioned.

The true center of the person becomes lost amid the distractions that consume him. He may forget why he got into the business in the first place. His priorities become misplaced, changing the nature of the whole project and affecting his life and the lives of those around him.

Relationships are the anchors that help provide direction in our lives. Because of the imbalance of priorities entrepreneurship requires, relationships suffer. Without care and attention, they become unnecessary casualties. The entrepreneur may abuse relationships by failing to keep promises and fulfill commitments.

Busy with the trivia of the business, he practices poor time management – working constantly expands to fill the time allowed and family time suffers. At the very time he needs it most the entrepreneur often finds himself discarding the emotional recharging that time with friends and family provides.

For me this became apparent one day when I realized that I was never really *there* for my kids, at least not in a way I could feel good about. I realized it was not my physical presence that was needed, but the real person inside, the father who smiled and was fully present and engaged in their lives.

I'll never forget the time where I became aware – really aware – of my habit of picking up the phone while playing with the kids and being wrapped up in a discussion on the phone while the kids were at my feet trying to get my attention. It seemed as though everything else was more important then simply being present in the moment, enjoying my time with my children.

Along with success, what also happens very often in the process is that the entrepreneur becomes someone else. He discards the role he began with and slides into the role he thinks is required of him. Associating with new peers, listening to poor advice, and believing flattery that supports his new self image can become a way of life. Seduced by the siren's song of success (or what he perceives success to be) decisions are based on reinforcing his self image, rather than what might be best for the business he commands.

The entrepreneur might change to fit in with his new relationships. He might decide to move to a bigger house, better neighborhood, or even another part of the world. He works to fulfill the expectations of his new acquaintances, rather than adhere to his own values. The preconceived notions of what he thinks he should do become the driving force for his actions.

The funny thing is that most of this happens in a state of unawareness, perhaps even the unwillingness to stop and really look in the mirror. Life has turned to a set of tasks with one goal after another on the horizon.

I've gotten so wrapped up in the day to day challenges that I found myself going after goals themselves. Perhaps it was the excitement of achievement, but one significant goal that I achieved was the purchase of a large dream house. I had gotten so wrapped up in this one goal that once I achieved it I discovered that it wasn't all that important to me anymore.

When I think back on what it took to get the house – all the planning, overcoming the obstacles – it seemed as though achieving it was just another goal. This was actually a turning point in my life, having achieved such a grand goal but feeling empty inside once I achieved it.

I remember clearly a friend and mentor in my life at the time mentioning to me that he had hoped that someday I would realize the gift I had – the passion and enthusiasm to move through the virtually impossible – and that I would put it to good use in the future. I know now that he meant serving others and not just in achieving material goals.

This is the true tragedy of the problems that the entrepreneur faces. Despite the physical challenges, he does everything he can to be successful, then finds that the dream is out of reach. The question becomes, *Where did the dream go?*

There are different answers to each situation. Maybe you simply lost sight of the dream. The dream may not have been realistic to begin with. Perhaps it wasn't the right dream for you, or that it wasn't as you expected.

If you find yourself in this situation, the sooner that you can realize it, redefine it, learn from it and begin again, the sooner you can restart movement toward your dream. The true entrepreneur knows this. Most successful entrepreneurs have had at least one venture fail before they found the right one. The process demands certain actions.

Realize it. Are you getting the results you wanted? Start early in learning to look at your end result and ask yourself if this is what you really want. Your answer to this should be either yes or no. Regardless of the answer, it's vital that you acknowledge where you are.

If you want to get anywhere, you can't possibly do it unless you know where you are at any given time. If you want to go to Nevada, your starting point determines your direction. You can't simply decide that you'll go "west" and expect to find your destination. If you're in Phoenix, Arizona, you'd simply wind up in California, and would have missed Nevada. Getting from point A to point B demands that you know where point A is.

It sometimes takes a lot of courage to accept where you really are. As an entrepreneur, you are there as a result of your own efforts. You may fight it; tell others how far you've gotten – there, getting there, almost there – but ultimately you are where you are.

Redefine it. The sooner you accept the fact that you are in the wrong place, the sooner you can ask the questions needed to make the right choices and move forward again. Do you need to try another avenue? Do you need to make changes in your business, your offering or your people?

There's no point in mourning the loss of the previous dream. After all, it isn't lost; it's merely been changed to reflect your new situation. Looking back at what might have been, or dwelling on mistakes you might have made, only holds you back.

Learn from it. More important is that you determine not to repeat the mistakes you made previously. Ultimately you really can't expect to get a different result by doing the same thing every time. (Insanity is doing the same thing over and over and expecting a different result.) Learning from your past decisions – whether mistakes or successes – is the one way that you can ensure that your next effort will be more successful than your last one.

Begin again. Eventually, regardless of previous disappointments, you have set sail one more time. It's your life, your goal. What alternative do you have? You have to live your life one way or another. The heart of the true entrepreneur beats faster when presented with opportunities. You were made to keep on trying when others have stopped.

CHAPTER TWO

Were You Prepared?

Those who go into business for themselves typically have a large number of positive attributes that contribute to their success. These people are almost universally ambitious, of course. Whether they're motivated by money, by the desire to create or driven to do something to change the world, ambition is the one common trait that they all have.

Other traits that entrepreneurs may have are confidence, courage, patience, discipline and endurance. All of these characteristics are necessary for someone to go into business for himself. These traits are also necessary for the business or endeavor to get off to a good start.

With all of these positive attributes, however, somewhere along the way many of them begin to question their decision to go into business. Their passion begins to wane and they are not quite sure what happened. It's almost as if they become trapped inside their own business. What was supposed to create freedom from a job has suddenly transformed into a job again - but this time one that you own.

One indicator that there may be trouble is that once you go into business for yourself you end up doing less and less of what you got into business for in the first place (at least for most people). Often you go into business because you can be better off on your own, make more money and have more control of your opportunities, but the main reason is that you can be independent and nobody is there to tell you what to do anymore – basically be your own boss. You like what you do and you like the idea of doing it your way.

That's how it starts, but eventually other burdensome responsibilities start to pile up. At a very minimum they require a lot of time to do – marketing, networking, invoicing, working out problems, hiring someone to help, management, and the list goes on.

Before you know it you're not doing what you went into business for in the first place. You're not having any fun, and the excitement and passion has drained out of you. The long hours start to wear on you and even if the money is great – which was such a great motivator at the beginning – it no longer seems quite as significant.

Although there are a number of reasons an individual may lose his passion for the business, here is a partial list of possible causes:

- They misjudge the importance of having a strategic plan for all areas of the business.

- They misjudge the severity of an absence of systems and lack the skills to develop and maintain these properly.

- They have an underdeveloped understanding of the roles and responsibilities of leadership and often get wrapped up in day-to-day operational functions to the detriment of great leadership.

• They lack essential management skills as well as adequate time to develop people.

• They lack the skills and perhaps even underestimate the importance of building and maintaining great customer service.

• They lack communication skills.

• They underestimate the importance of understanding basic financial strategies, as well as properly comprehending financial statements, cash flow and how these aid in the financial stability of the business.

Strategic Plan

The strategic plan is vital for any business to succeed and prosper. All stakeholders benefit when the leader has a clear idea of what the business is about. Customers, employees, vendors and partners all feel much more comfortable when the leader has a sense of mission and a path mapped out to take them where they want to go.

Of course, one of the main people to benefit is the entrepreneur himself. This one step – creating a strategic plan for your business – can be the difference in whether your business succeeds or fails. Planning is simply preparation, and starting a business or any other project without preparation is a formula for disaster.

I like to remind myself of the following phrase: "How can you know where you're going when you don't know where you are?" This question pops into my head from time to time reminding me to look around and make sure I have a plan in place whenever things aren't going as well as I would like. In the haste of a busy day, weeks or even months anyone can become off target. It is important to stop and make sure things aren't misaligned and make corrections if needed.

Almost any business can make a profit when times are good. Those that have a good plan, however, make more in good times. What's even better is that they can not only survive, but make a profit during tough economic times. Those without a plan fall by the wayside.

My IT company has weathered many storms. We've gotten past the internet bubble and watched a lot of businesses tumble. Many of them were our clients at the time. The events of 9/11 also threw a pretty good wrench into the world of business. Here, too, several of our clients went out of business.

Then along came the real estate collapse that really caught many people by surprise. I saw many businesses fall and a lot of doubt swept the nation and continues even today. This event really had a worldwide effect and I hear it from many people I know throughout different parts of the world. We have been able to hang on not only due to my commitment as a business owner but also due to the willingness to learn and grow from every experience, good or bad. The same can be said of my staff – who are an important part of everyday business. Looking into the mirror has become an important part of our day. Where we had not planned before, we now plan. The value is very clear.

With a plan in place, the business owner can set up systems so he doesn't have to do so much himself – he has leverage. When all the employees know the direction that the business owner wants to go they have an idea of the types of decisions they need to make, actions they need to take, and steps to get things done without the owner having to oversee every move.

The Importance of a System

After you have the right people in place to join your team of committed individuals the next step, which is absolutely essential, is to develop a system. It is a system which will make it all come together and ultimately give you the freedom you are looking for.

A system will set your people up for success. It will guide them through the process of how your business works and how things must be done in order to achieve its primary objective. In short, a system is that which holds the processes and procedures that enables your company to achieve the result it is out to deliver in the marketplace. It contains the specific steps as well as a specific order someone has to follow to deliver a very specific result.

People often underestimate how valuable a well thought-out set of processes can be for a company trying to deliver a consistent quality of service or product. I know this from my quality management days and by having the personal experience in the early days at SIC Consulting. I didn't have enough time to build a system and thought I could get by without one because the company was really small.

It was in the years following when I realized that developing and using a system applies not only to medium and larger companies, but small ones too. Eventually I realized the sometimes painful fact (by doing the opposite) that a properly planned business might have the ability to achieve an extraordinary result, but it is best done right from the start. Otherwise it will need to have a major, often painful, overhaul in the future if it is to survive over time, especially if the founders ever want to step away from it, sell it, or even to simply just get away for a real vacation.

In fact, if your business is to ever have a real value to the marketplace in the event an owner wishes to sell his interest in their company to a third party, having a system in place will give it a higher value, often called a multiplier. I have seen many business owners end up having to stick around several years as an employee of their own company because the business could not continue to function without its owner, who really is the business. These owners often ended up with far less then they could have.

Typically more mature companies buy out smaller companies this way. Mature companies often come armed with a system and aim to integrate the acquired company into an existing system. If you want to increase the value of your business, then it is advisable to build a system around your business – otherwise the only value will be your client base. It often takes two to five years to slowly build a system around a company – one process at a time. It's a bit of a process; however persons looking to acquire a business will pay a higher price when the business is built around a set of processes with clearly defined roles and responsibilities. In short, the business can stand on its own feet and have enough people in it to perform all basic functions and not have the entire operation hinged on a single person or owner.

I had such a business and I was approached by a company which looked to expand by acquiring other small companies. The first time I considered it I really got involved in the process, trying to understand how this was supposed to work and what made the most sense for me. I met with various business owners, seeking those who had already done it to see how their experiences were and what they felt worked and what they would do differently if they had to do it all over again.

I learned a lot during this time and ended up negotiating a value I felt was right for me with the company that wanted to merge to create a larger new company. I ended up not doing this deal because in the process of learning about company valuation I realized that my company was going to be undervalued due to lack of systems not being built out and detailed enough at the time.

In my case I would have reduced my one hundred percent control of my company to about twenty-five to thirty percent. Although I was excited about the team of committed partners I would have, along with the increased earning potential, I felt this deal wasn't going to be right for me.

It didn't match the ultimate direction and vision I had in my mind through the many years of being in the IT service business.

In many ways it was hard to let that go, as I was seeking out business partners to take the company to a whole new level, because at that time I felt I wasn't able to do this without other partners who would be more invested than an employee might.

The second time I was approached from a company, I was offered a set buy-out price. They weren't interested in working with me as a partner, and I wouldn't be able to compete in the same market for a number of years. The offer came at a time when I was a bit burned-out, and I contemplated taking it.

This all happened at a time when I was simply overwhelmed and still had oversight on just about every department in my company and I knew I needed help in the area of key management. I was tired of running this company on my own, tired of dealing with all the employee issues and tired of carrying all the financial risk. It was just too much and it all just didn't seem worth the effort anymore.

It didn't take me long, however, to realize that I would be selling out short and doing it only to get some much needed relief. I knew that it would be only temporary relief because it wasn't going to be the right thing to do. It also didn't make financial sense. This is when I made yet another commitment to make further adjustments to my business.

What I didn't realize at the time was that this situation would ultimately bring me to where I stand today. I can accept the way things are and the way people are. My expectations for people had to change before I could become successful in moving beyond a place I had been stuck in for many years.

Today I am grateful for the way things went. I have become a better leader and a better person in the process. It is what grounds me today.

A few words about franchises as their structures help display the value and presence of systems:

A franchise is nothing more than a system consisting of an idea put on paper. It is the reason many business owners or investors choose this route when going into business for themselves. A franchise is well thought out, developed down to every detail. Everything from how the business is going to look and feel, the equipment to be used, the items to be purchased, processes and roles that keep the business running - all are coordinated to make sure the franchise is in alignment with the larger company's goals. All this contributes to why franchises have a much higher survival rate over time and with a much more predictable revenue.

Franchises definitely have their place in the world. My own passion lies in creating a business from scratch, or I would choose the franchise route instead of creating my own.

If you decide to start your own business, determining and developing a system is best started before you even open the doors. A business without a system is like a ship without a rudder! Such a business will struggle over time, have unpredictable growth and revenue, and challenge both owners and staff. A system is ultimately what will make or break your business, or possibly even you.

The Importance of Leadership

There are many differences between a manager and a leader. The leader is more like a director in a movie. He directs, guides and oversees a production. The leader carries the ultimate responsibility to make sure key business objectives are met.

The manager, on the other hand, is responsible for the outcome of individual projects and the coordination of a team.

He is someone who makes sure key processes are performed in a certain way.

The key difference, however, is that the leader has a vision and communicates that vision to his team. The vision is more than the strategic plan. It's the idea of what the business itself is trying to do, and what the entrepreneur – the leader – wants the business to accomplish in the marketplace.

The leader understands the importance of his role in the fulfillment of the company's primary objective and serves as an anchor to the values and principles that guide him and, by definition, the company that he has started. He has the ability to clearly communicate and pave the way for his people to fulfill the company's vision. He challenges, guides and encourages his team to grow and reach new heights. The leader helps navigate the team through difficult situations. This means that the leader can't get caught up doing everything himself. Someone needs to steer the ship and its people – this is his main function. He needs to keep an overview on all aspects of the operation. He detects deficiencies in the systems and people, and sets in place corrections when needed. He cannot do all this when he's doing too much within the business – being involved with invoicing, bookkeeping, managing projects, personnel issues, and all the other various details that make an organization work.

All of these are important to a business, of course. But the leader makes sure that everyone understands what is *most* important in their individual roles. This is the reason that the best leaders also tend to be the best delegators. They focus on the bigger picture and have others perform key processes that make the business work. This leads us to the next point.

Developing People

The person starting a business may have a blind spot when it comes to developing people. He is driven and motivated, and believes that others are also. However, without the same motivation and vision, those who work with or for the entrepreneur may not put the same energy into the enterprise.

Putting energy into training and developing people helps them increase their skill set, which also helps with their personal growth – they begin to value themselves because of their increased abilities and the attention paid to them. Increasing their skills also helps the entrepreneur maximize profits, since fewer resources (people) are required when each participant is properly trained.

Having developed people also helps the entrepreneur prepare for success on the next level. The more responsibility he can assign or delegate to others, the fewer tasks that require his personal presence. Without the distraction of certain aspects of the business, he can focus his energy on those activities that prepare him for moving to a higher level.

This is why the entrepreneur puts in so many hours at the beginning of starting a business or a project. When something is new he is the only one that has a clear idea of *what* needs to be done and *how* it needs to be done. If he spends a large portion of that time developing and training his people they eventually become able to do the individual tasks, and he can concentrate on doing the most important things he needs to do to further grow the business.

Where do entrepreneurs go wrong in developing people? Once again, lack of planning can hurt. Without a systematic method of both training and evaluating skill level, the trainer has no sure way of knowing who will be successful handling certain tasks and who will not. Similarly, a lack of focus can create personnel who are well-trained in some areas but poorly trained in others.

Without structure and focus, training can be hit-or-miss.

Another trap is lack of knowledge of the individual. Every person learns (and wants to learn) at different levels, at different speeds, in different ways. Trying to fit a "one size fits all" philosophy onto development ignores the reality of development. Your expectations may also be incorrect. From some people you may expect too much, and from others too little. The only way you can adjust your expectations is by knowing the individual you are developing.

The responsibility for developing your people will always fall to you. A major mistake is assuming that you can delegate the responsibility for developing your people to someone else. You may have instructors, trainers or others whose job is to train, but your trainers will also need your development to make sure that they are competent at *their* tasks.

Although you may use such a level of instruction as a tool, the end result – fully-developed and trained people – is something you have to properly design and set in place, and is your responsibility.

Customer Service

For a business to thrive, it must answer this question: Who is our customer? The type of business will define much of that, of course. A store that sells big ticket items will appeal to more affluent customers. A restaurant that features a clown will appeal to families with small children. Addressing the needs of a particular group is much simpler and more manageable than trying to be all things to all people.

For example, if your business caters to young single adults you will design your advertising and marketing toward media that appeal to that group, perhaps using the internet or social networking sites. If your service is geared to seniors, other media may be more effective, perhaps radio or newspaper. Knowing who your business serves is the only way to properly contour your efforts.

All of this is useless, however, if you fail at providing top notch service to the customers who, literally or figuratively, walk in your door. On the one hand, taking care of your own customers will ensure that you are executing the mission and vision that you have for your company. With the general decline of proper customer service in our culture today providing exceptional customer service will also separate your business from your competitors.

Poor customer service has almost become a cliché. Most people have had the experience of going through the drive through at a fast food restaurant only to discover when they were miles down the road that they received the wrong order. This is a frustrating experience.

Imagine if your employees were trained to provide service to your customers every step of the way, until the customer decided that everything was good. Can you see how your customers would not only be happy with your company, but also tell others of the high level of service?

At SIC Consulting, Inc. we spent a lot of time in this area. After 14 years in business, we learned the tremendous value in taking care of our customers. In fact, we sought out partnerships, rather than simply someone to "do business" with. Grounded in our value, we understood our business and brought along an entire team of committed individuals. We took the time to study our market and the challenges businesses had in and around information technology, as well as their challenges with IT vendors or even their own IT staff. This approach had a high value to our client and was at the foundation of the win-win relationship we aimed to establish with every client.

The concept of "partnering" is where we created a rather unique approach to proper care and thoroughness to every client. Our aim was to become an integral part of their operation, an extension of their staff, and to ensure that our clients felt the care that is at our company's core. We achieved this by taking time to get to know their business, how it operated and functioned. To guide our team in this process, we created an entire concept around this goal, directed by a carefully designed and ever expanding quality management system.

Armed with this information we are able to align their technology needs to their business objectives and make the focus their business, rather than their technology. We believe this creates an end result that is extremely desirable, and which very few competitors will be able to accomplish.

Communication

Another major pitfall for those going into business is having poor communication skills. Effective communication is vital for the transmission of information and instructions. If you have poor communication, then you needlessly expend energy merely trying to get something done.

For a variety of reasons, ambiguous messages, failure to listen, not accounting for "noise", the communications skills of many businesspeople are inadequate for what they want to accomplish. Unfortunately, communicating is something that many people take for granted and they often overestimate their skill level. Consequently, they never address what can be a serious handicap in their development.

The person who goes into business who also concentrates on effective communication is ahead of his competition. Whether it's when training employees, setting expectations with vendors, or discovering your customers' needs, an effective communicator will always have the edge over the poor communicator.

Financial Intelligence

Having financial oversight on your business can make or break your company, as well as your dreams. It is essential to spend some time understanding your numbers and how they relate to your business. At a very basic level you will want to have an accurate overview of your fixed and variable costs as well your areas of income. It is advisable to use an accounting program to properly track this information. Accounting programs make it easy to maintain a regular overview through your profit and loss reports as well as your balance sheet. Spend some time getting to know these reports, as many people going into business don't even know how to read these basic reports. Armed with this information you will be able to have proper oversight on your cash flow and better project your overall financial status, allowing you to seek corrections when they are required. It will also guide you in proper record-keeping essential to your operation as well as your financial obligations. Note: Hiring a qualified bookkeeper is absolutely essential early on in your business.

At a more advanced level, having financial oversight and control of your numbers in more detail allows you to better align your company's resources to attain a more controlled predictable result. Such an example could be your income statement where you break down your various income streams ranging from products to services.

By understanding which specific income streams are growing, versus shrinking, you can either increase your marketing efforts in a specific product or service or realize that it may be better to drop one.

If you don't have that kind of oversight as well as the ability to review historic income numbers, your company will spend its time and effort in the wrong direction and thus become less profitable, or worse yet, fail. This is increasingly important as you grow and need to maintain visibility over many products and services as well as various departments. The lack of this level of visibility will greatly stagger your growth, so start when you are small.

With all that I've mentioned, however, disappointments and frustrations still crop up in the life of someone starting his own business. Here are some statements I've heard over the years from people in business, things they tend to focus on that get them stuck:

The economy is really tough. It's true, the economy does go up and down and sometimes what has worked for years suddenly stops working. This is where so many get stuck, give up or simply become victims of circumstances.

Everything in life has its ups and downs. It is best to be ready for shifts when they happen and not to fight them. This takes practice, but ultimately requires a perception or attitude shift. Otherwise you are lost and really don't have a chance.

On the other hand, the person who learns to accept those things that he cannot change and gets into a habit of embracing change when the opportunity arises will quickly move to higher ground. Why? While most people are stuck and not doing anything, the few who take advantage of new circumstances move into the lead. There is minimal competition in this area.

In summary, a bad economy often offers the most opportunity. If you look back into history most of our innovation has come during these times.

You really can't find quality people (workers) these days. Yes, people are difficult and rarely do people behave the way you would like for them to. On the other hand, what's your alternative? Being negative about people really doesn't move you forward either. To be successful in the long haul you have to master working with people.

This is another area of surrender. Learn to be a leader, someone who refuses to be cynical and who refuses to criticize people. The right people will come if you deserve them. Good people don't work for people that don't respect other people. You just can't retain good people and you won't get the best out of them. It just doesn't work.

In the end, nobody is you or thinks like you do. The ones that do are often your competitors and will never work for you. Why should they? Where is their incentive? You make most of the money (and of course you work for it too!) but don't expect someone who is not in your shoes to ever see that.

How can they? It is not within their experience and they can only look at it from their own perspective. They will never truly understand, and they don't need to. Unless you've actually done it, people see only what they are able and want to see. Save yourself the time and energy trying to convince them. It won't work and it will leave you and your employees frustrated.

There are too many competitors in our market. I believe amateurs compete and true professionals create, team up and collaborate. I like a phrase I heard that goes something like this: *You will always get paid in direct proportion to the service you provide to others.* There is always enough for everyone. You have to come from a place of abundance and know that a good product or service is always in need.

In fact there are many businesses in the same city, sometimes on the same street. One fails, the other thrives. How does that happen? It's because one business does the same thing a certain way. It may be in the same market but it does it just a little better. It could be in the way they greet customers, it could be in their follow up, or in their overall level of service.

So often it is just that the person providing the service is a pleasant person to be around, someone that makes the customer feel good. It's really not that complicated because when you think about it, it's just simple human satisfaction and how a person feels about another that makes the experience worthwhile. A smile and a great attitude contribute greatly to your success!

Our prices are too high. This is a good one. Personally, I don't compete in price. My focus is in the *value* I provide. It is a choice for me, as when you compete in price you have a lot more competition.

When you compete in price your margins are low. The people you deal with are usually focused primarily on price and do not place much value on the product or service you provide. Don't do this to yourself. Especially when building up a small business it is essential to develop your own unique value to your customer. Trying to compete with a Best Buy or Wal-Mart does not make much sense. Most of us just want to get paid a fair price for the service we provide and go to bed knowing we did our best and are respected in what it is we do. To do this you have to differentiate yourself. It sounds a lot more complicated than it really is, but it does require some stepping back to figure out. You've got to figure out what it is you do that you are really good at. What is it that someone needs? How can you best deliver them the end result in the most efficient manner? A great book that I recommend is *The Rainmaker: The Rules for Getting and Keeping Customers and Clients*, by Jeffrey J. Fox.

I have to do everything myself. In this case, you feel you have to do things yourself because others just can't do it right. There is some truth to this from one perspective, but at the same time it is also a perspective that gets you stuck and greatly limits your ability to become successful. Simply stated, you are only one person and you only have so much time.

Think of it this way: if you are 100% utilized you will eventually make X dollars. By working extra hard (at night or weekends) you may get up to 120% or even 200% utilization at the best of times. It is then that you will make a nice amount of money. You are usually ecstatic at first because, after all, this is partly what makes it all worth it. But in time, you will burn out. It is then when you will realize (the hard way) that it really isn't worth it and it will often leave many cynical and frustrated once again.

Another way to look at it: If you can get others to help you (say 4 people) at only 75% utilization, plus your own 100%, your company can reach 400% utilization. The point here is your total utilization far exceeds that of your personal capacity alone. That is what leverage is all about. Ultimately you will personally end up with compensation of about 150-200% depending on the efficiency in your business. But you're only working at 100% rather than at a burn-out mode of 150% and beyond, which is often the performance level of most entrepreneurs. This is just an example and often just the beginning. A fully leveraged business yields an entirely different and exceedingly higher financial reward than shown in the above example. It has to do with looking at your business with the mindset of an "investor" rather than a "self-employed owner". An "investor" looks at his business from a broad and slightly detached view, focusing on systems, and how to create leverage, while a "self-employed owner" is often more personally identified and involved with the business, spending more personal time on day-to-day issues and thus less focus is placed on how to fully leverage the business model.

I know it's a hard thing to imagine, but trust me, it works and I learned the hard way. I always found proof that others couldn't help in the business as I needed them to, so I did many things myself and it took me some time to realize that it is me that paid the price. I used to frustrate my mentors when I was raging about how incompetent my team was, complaining about how I had to do "everything" myself, and on and on.

I laugh now because my mentors were so right. Well, you live and learn. I learned and today I actually make more money than I did when I was working twice the hours in the past when I was wrecking myself, with no time for family, friends, or hobbies. This went on for many years! Does this sound familiar to you or is this still ahead of you?

Tip: Learn to accept that nobody will do things as you do but if they do a part of what you do and you can multiply it (leverage it), you will be so much happier and so will your customers, your family and friends because being around a wigged out business owner really isn't a pretty picture. In the end you may lose some of them along the way: customers, employees, friends and family.

Nobody really cares, just me. This is another one of those victim statements. Of course people care, just not in the same way as you do. Again, why should they? Live with it.

The best thing you can do is don't be selfish. Think of a win-win for everyone. If you have employees or plan to have them, figure out a way to compensate them as much as you can. Depending on where they are in life it may be more money, it may be time off, a trip for two to Las Vegas or Hawaii or some other idea or gift.

Find out what it is they like, what gets them going. Get to know the people that work for you. Ask them. The sheer fact that you take an interest in their life (care about them) will make them care about you. It really is an inside to outside approach. Don't expect them to care if you really don't care. Find a way to motivate each individual and learn what is important to them.

Create this atmosphere and you will develop a good workforce which will be noticed by your customers and greatly contribute to your company's success, or for that matter, *all* success in every area of life! Don't make the mistake and underestimate this.

Laws and regulations are killing us. Don't fight it; just find the best way to deal with it. Laws and regulations *help* your life too so just surrender and work hard to not let this be a hurdle.

In fact, you can turn this into an advantage by learning more about it; perhaps even by creating a value around the fact that you comply to certain regulations. Maintain knowledge for the protection of your client or employees.

Customer demands are just unrealistic. Yes, they often are, but then put yourself in their place. All they want is for things to work. They don't know your profession and lack the expertise to understand what it takes to make all you do really work. The best thing you can do is listen to them, and I mean *listen* to them. That means not trying to convince them of your perspective, which they ultimately don't understand and may even come to resent you.

Listen, learn and develop the understanding that they don't have all the pieces and that they often just know they want things to work and don't see why things are that hard. You've got to have the patience to work with this and respond with a calm and clear voice, never frustrated. Work at this very hard and it will change their perception and create an enormous amount of respect for you personally and the company for which you represent.

It also makes them come back, buy more, and refer you to other customers. Even when they choose to go elsewhere, if you treated them fairly and well, one day they may come back and be one of your best customers. Don't burn any bridges, ever!

We have the wrong customers, and need new ones. There is something to be said about having the right customers. When you're first beginning you often just aren't that picky about who buys from you, but in time you may realize that not all customers are worth having.

This is not because you are "better" than them, but simply because they are not in alignment with where you have grown as a business or even as an individual.

There is nothing wrong with that. So when that time comes, what is important is that you know what that right customer looks like and to be absolutely clear why!

If you can't answer these questions then you have some work ahead of you. Some soul searching may be necessary. You need to know what your ideal client looks like. Even more importantly, you need to know what it is that you will offer them *specifically* that is of real value to them.

You are the one who has to be clear and in complete alignment. Otherwise you will simply not attract those "right customers" – it just doesn't work that way. They will come when you are ready!

There just isn't enough time to do everything. Get some help! If you don't have any or can't afford any, then do less! Less really is more. Doing one thing well is much better than doing many things average. Prioritize and add more things later, when you have completed the most important things first, or have more money or resources.

We need more money. Always start with what you can afford. It is easier that way! Nobody says you have to do everything all at once. Most millionaires didn't make it overnight; they made it one step at a time.

If you want to play a bigger game then get some help. Create a plan and make yourself attractive. Find some partners that complement your strengths and talents and if money is an issue find an investor.

However, getting investors involved is a whole different ball game and you will need to be prepared because investors expect you to hit your targets and they will hold you accountable. If you fail to meet expectations they may eventually pull back out, leaving your business in a free fall.

It's a great option and something worth exploring if you're really ready for this level, but be aware that it comes with its own set of risks.

In the end, don't make lack of money an excuse not to do anything. There are many ways to do things on an economic scale. I started my business in my dining room and eventually expanded to my bedroom where I had to put my copy machine, as I didn't have enough room on my desk. I made my own flyers, printed them out, drove around and dropped them in mail slots, picked up the phone and made calls using the yellow pages. I gained a few accounts, was completely dedicated to servicing them, and the referrals started flowing in.

I now have a defined purpose, in developing a company with a mission, a staff of people to support my vision, and some really great clients that all contribute to the fulfillment of my dream. I am well on my way to creating the kind of liberty I seek – time to do the things I enjoy and are important to me in my life, and the money to support my lifestyle. To think it started with absolutely nothing but me, my vision and my belief and discipline to do the things I knew I had to do every day!

Achieving success can be a hard, lonely road – but it doesn't have to be. Working hard and working smart can make starting your own business fulfilling and rewarding, without sacrificing the rest of your life. Your aim from the start should be to use your enterprise to add to the quality of your life.

CHAPTER THREE

Preparation of a Dream

Do you know where you're going? It's pretty important to know where it is that you're headed, because if you don't know, then how can you expect *anyone* else to know where you are going? A successful leader must first carve out the road. He must define it and know what it is going to look like in order to be successful telling others what to do and how they can assist you in getting where you want to go. "No destination and no direction" is just not a realistic success plan.

So where are you going? Do you have your goal defined? Is it really clear to you?

Before you answer, it may prove helpful to consider a few things. For one thing, what you think your goal is may not be the right goal for you at all.

In my own experience, I have realized that there are different types of goals, and each of them has its own place. For example, you may have personal goals and you may have business or professional goals. Most of us have to deal with the two worlds. If these two worlds are not in alignment, then things just don't seem to come together.

I lived in Frankfurt, Germany during my early childhood then moved to the USA with my family. I spent summers in Germany until the 1980's, when I moved from California back to Germany to study. I went to school as an apprentice to become a tool and die maker in Regensburg, Germany. I studied hard, worked hard, and after I passed all my exams I thought I was ready to go into the world and do something with my life. For the next few years I stayed at the same company where I had done my apprenticeship. I deepened my skills acquired during my apprenticeship and I was finally able to make a decent paycheck.

I enjoyed the work, using AutoCAD and CAD/CAM systems. I designed form tools for a variety of industries and got into 3D modeling. Although this was interesting, I went back to school a few years later and acquired my degree as a mechanical engineer. While working in that industry, I realized that I really enjoyed working with computers.

I eventually decided to go to Frankfurt and join my cousin, who had just finished his PhD in the area of engineering and economics, and a couple of other graduates to start a consulting company.

Here was my first chance to use my advanced education, and to put my skills to the test. Together we built up a consulting company that worked with companies in the design and implementation of quality management systems. We also helped companies in building out their environmental management systems as an additional area of expertise. It was a blast and it gave me a chance to put my entrepreneurial spirit to the test and see where it took me.

I enjoyed all the benefits such a job gave me. I made good money and was able to go out and buy things and do many of the things I had deprived myself of as a student. Instead of scraping by financially, eating a lot of pasta, rice and potatoes to save money, I was able to enjoy life more.

Years later, in 1997, I decided to pack up my bags and head back to the United States. After spending ten years in Germany I missed the warmer weather I once knew in California. Coupled with further dreams to build a new company, it was time to go.

It didn't take long for me to get things rolling in California. After arriving I first intended to expand on the original concept we already had in place at SIC Consulting GmbH in Germany. This is why we carried a similar company name – that being SIC Consulting, Inc. I started doing some work in the area of quality management consulting and trying to figure out how the market in the United States was different from that in Europe. Within the year I decided to take on another focus and headed into technology consulting. It was an area I had a lot of interest and knowledge in.

I helped companies I consulted with to better leverage technology and became the technician that implemented everything. I began growing SIC Consulting, Inc. from there. This company gave me even more power to further build my financial goals.

Somewhere along the line I decided that buying a car was a good goal, so I did it. I also began to make other purchases, "things" that I had not been able to buy before. Yes, I was in heaven, or so I thought.

Of course, I had to make payments, and that meant working harder and longer. Eventually I was working so much that I was not able to enjoy all the things I had bought.

One day I realized that I was only spending about twenty percent of my time doing things I really enjoyed, and the rest of the time was spent doing things that just needed to be done and is part of owning a business.

I loved riding my motorcycle, yet I was working so much that I wasn't able to ride as often as I wanted to. The same went for my convertible that I bought to enjoy sunny California.

Somewhere along the line I realized that I didn't have much time for my family. The nights at the office had gotten longer and longer. Living at my job was not what I wanted out of life – I wanted to go camping with my son, take my daughter on a convertible ride along the coast, have date nights and picnics with my wife, and do a million other things in life that I was missing out on. My relationships with my family and friends were also suffering.

It took me a while, but eventually I began to define what I wanted to do outside of work, and my goals changed. Instead of spending every waking minute earning money, I started to pull back. Instead of having to control every aspect of a project, I began to train and trust other people. Whereas before I had felt that I needed to do everything myself and micro-manage others, I worked to develop my trust in others and in their abilities.

In the process of working with other people, I discovered that I loved developing others and helping them grow. I wanted other people to be successful, and to also lead balanced lives that maximized their happiness in life.

This added pressure to me to develop more balance in my own life. How could I guide others to do what I was not doing myself? How could I lead if I was not a good example, one that others would be willing to follow?

I realized that my goals had not been the correct ones. My real goal should have been to enjoy life more fully, using my business as a tool rather than becoming a slave to earning a wage. By imagining a larger overall picture, I found that I had many more ways of enjoying my life and that they corresponded with helping others enjoy *their* lives.

What happened was that I began to realize that I had a *purpose* in life, one for which I felt I was born. I loved helping people and knew I could have an impact on their happiness and satisfaction in life, and I seemed to have a knack for it. My particular abilities and strengths came together in such a way that allowed me to create a new and exciting purpose in life - one that energized and fulfilled me.

The goals that I had set previously were based on momentary urges – I had more money, so I had to have more stuff. My *goal* had become to earn more money, simply so that I could afford more stuff. I thought I was living a good life, but instead I had sacrificed the things I most enjoyed for all that "stuff."

Knowing where you are going begins with examining yourself and discovering your own purpose in life. As I discovered, if you head in a direction that is different from your purpose, it's like swimming upstream. If you're really energetic, you can be successful, but ultimately the greater satisfaction and enjoyment of your time will be when you go with the flow of your inner being.

This is why I suggest spending time seriously considering where you're going. Stop and ask yourself if what you are doing today will give you more of what you really want tomorrow, a month from now, a year from now, and beyond. Going in a direction that is in alignment with who you are is what will ultimately give you meaning and fulfillment in life.

Years can go by while you're busy being busy – all the while headed in the wrong direction.

Only you can decide if you're headed in the right direction. Just staying busy, even with a plan, can leave you feeling frustrated and empty in the long haul. Working in alignment with your purpose in life makes everything smoother, and success that much sweeter.

Each of us has unique gifts and strengths that enable us to do things that most other people can't do. Those gifts and strengths are what make us individuals, separate and unique from everyone else. They also are part of what makes up our unique purpose in life. However, you can't know your own gifts and strengths unless you examine yourself, and continue to do so on an ongoing basis.

What I'm talking about is taking an inventory of your own particular attributes. To get the most out of life, it's been my experience that you have more power and greater satisfaction if you do everything you can to work with your strengths. That means you have to do some self-study and find out what your own strengths are.

The most common feedback we often get is negative. A child turns in a test and incorrect answers are marked with a big red X. At work you are doing fine and don't hear anything but then you make a mistake and the boss makes sure to give you an earful.

All of this negativity is the opposite of what you want, but naturally people tend to gravitate to what is going wrong rather than what is going right. Remember, you're looking for your strengths. That feedback is harder to get, but will be the most revealing. Ask those around you to name your strengths, and you may get some surprised looks at first, because people are not used to thinking in terms of strengths.

There are also some good books out that can help you discover your strengths. One in particular that I like is *Strengths Finder 2.0* by Tom Rath, based on research by the Gallup organization.

In my own case, it was self-study that opened my eyes.

Even with all my success, my lack of fulfillment frightened me. I knew that there had to be more to life. It was when I opened up, when I committed to actually improving myself that I realized that my previous successes kept me from achieving the results I really wanted.

Looking back now in the many years of building an IT company, I realize that my life was out of balance. I had somehow been diverted from my most important goals, and I knew I had to make adjustments.

Expanding my awareness of what I actually wanted out of life helped me in my interactions with clients, my staff, and with my friends and family. I recognized that I had some core competencies that I really enjoyed working with. Once I decided to focus on those competencies – my strengths, my talents – everything changed. I can honestly say that each day was so much more fulfilling. I became amazed at how much my communication skills developed, and how interactions that used to lead to arguments or conflict, became easier to navigate through. I also learned to help others navigate those same situations.

My focus, which had been almost exclusively on my work, changed to the really important things in my life, like my family. I resolved to spend less time on the parts of my business that I agonized over, and put more of my energies into those parts that played to my strengths.

I also learned to better manage my weaknesses. Some tasks I found difficult or unpleasant to do because my strengths lay elsewhere. I learned the value of delegating those to others. What

I also discovered in the process is that my weaknesses were indeed other people's strengths, and so I began to study the art of delegation.

At work I made sure that I worked on those parts which used my strengths and which were enjoyable. The rest I delegated or decided were not needed. I realized that my business, to a large extent, can actually run without me. This freed up my time and my energy so that I could concentrate on improving the quality of the business itself and the time that I spent with my family.

I made it a priority to spend less time at work and more time with my family. What I found is that when I stepped back and took a hard look at my life, I had been acting as though my business and my personal lives were in conflict. The exact opposite was true. When I concentrated on what was really important to me, my business goals and my personal goals began to fit together.

My experience showed me the importance of having flexibility in a plan. When we start to set goals and devise plans, we make the best decisions we can based on the information we have at the time, and our life situation. What makes designing a plan truly successful is the ability to take new information and new situations into account, and adjust the plan accordingly.

In my own case, making "time with my family" a top priority changed many of my other goals. By changing how I did things – adjusting my *plan* – I was able to spend more time with them and also discover the great potential that existed in my company and in my employees.

Stepping back from my business allowed me to better see gaps in the business. I could concentrate on areas where the business needed improvement. Ever since then I have made it a habit to step back and take a look at the "big picture" to see where we can improve on a regular basis.

Doing this in my own life made me realize how much I enjoyed doing it, and I began to help friends with some of their own business and professional involvements. I was able to share my experience, insights and energies with others.

Slowly I discovered that helping others was something I sincerely enjoyed.

I can now *focus* a lot of my energy on how I, and any business I lead, can add real value to the communities we serve that extend beyond a "for-profit" business. I am now focusing also on aspects of social responsibility. It is a new world for me and I'm enjoying many aspects of it already.

Being able to work *on* a business instead of working *in* a business has made all the difference in the world to me. I now enjoy the creative process of building businesses. I get to create a better product and service. Together with my team I now build stronger companies, ones that are founded on a solid foundation and grounded in a defined purpose. I am also devoting more attention on the personal and professional development of my staff to help them reach new heights and balance in their life.

To balance my own life, I now I have taken more trips with my wife and children (once we spent five weeks visiting my relatives in Italy over the holidays, as well as spending summers in Germany.) Whenever I come back from these trips I am refreshed and better able to engage in the high-level activities that every business requires to prosper.

One of the most important lessons that I have learned is that the best way to find success is to imagine the end result and then work backwards from there. When I started my businesses I was younger and full of energy. I built them brick by brick, based on my immediate needs or perceptions. I was successful to a degree, but I missed a lot of opportunities and wasted a lot of energy.

I find it sad when asking people what they would do if they won 10 million dollars today and most say they would quit their job that instant and do something completely different. I know we all have responsibilities, and a career change or doing something else doesn't come without challenges.

However, the price we pay staying where we are is often too high if it means not living a happy and fulfilled life, and so often we take it out on others as we interact with the world around us. I believe some deeper self-reflection can go a long way in making a more conscious choice. If you're going to spend 8+ hours a day at "work", which is a big part of your life, why do something that you can't wait to get away from? You owe it to yourself, your co-workers or team, your organization, and your family and friends to make a different choice – a more conscious choice.

When I became a husband and father, and a bit older, this all helped me focus on what was important. Spending time with my family and friends, and sharing what I have learned and what I see in the world we live in, became the "end result" that I wanted. I worked back from that desired result, and devised systems and approaches to help me achieve the liberty I wanted. While making those changes, I am grateful that I was able to see the untapped potential in my company, in my employees, and in myself. Today any business I am involved in are the "vehicles" to my goals and vision of financial liberty. Financial liberty to me means I can do more of what I want to do everyday - and have the means to do it. The equation for prospering both professionally and personally I believe is as follows:

Going into business for yourself, or engaging in helping one prosper and grow ("vehicle")

+

Finding something you love to do that has purpose beyond yourself ("purpose")

+

Defining clearly your own dreams and desires ("clarity")

+

Working hard and systematically to create true value to those you serve ("value")

+

Having gratitude for each step that gets you closer to your end result ("gratitude")

=

Personal fulfillment and liberty

CHAPTER FOUR

The Leadership Vision

Before taking action to achieve success, I've found that it often helps if you make your first step one of reflection and self analysis. This "inside-out" approach can help you make better decisions, ensure that any steps you take are in the right direction, and guide you toward looking at situations with a more enlightened point of view.

It's tempting to want to skip this step, and "just get on with it." Somewhere down the line there comes a point where you need to learn to really look at yourself. I think it's a part of becoming more mature in what we do as human beings. As we have more experiences, we learn more about what is important to us.

What happens, though, is that in the midst of a busy day we tend to get caught up in tons of "busy" activities. At first they appear important but if you take a couple of steps back you will often see that they really are just that -- "busy activities" that end up consuming your days, months and even years. What's worse is that these distractions -- which seem so important at the time -- often have very little to do with your bigger goals.

That's why self analysis is so important. Only by looking inside yourself can you find what truly makes you happy, and what really matters to you the most. In the end, you would only excel at something you are really passionate about doing and when it sits really close to your core values. Discovering your most basic beliefs, values and visions is the key to achieving lifelong success and personal satisfaction.

When you find what you were meant to do – your *purpose* – and you feel it in your bones, you wake up excited every day, eager to achieve that purpose. This is when you recognize that you are really ready and on the right road. Is this how you get up every morning now? Or do you dread getting up and find yourself saying "Oh no, it's Monday", or perhaps "Thank God it's Friday". If these or similar thoughts come on a regular basis you may want to start figuring out what would make you excited about each and every day.

Discovering your purpose and mission in life is a very personal thing. In fact, you are the only person in the world who can do the job. If you're not clear about your mission, then who else would be? How *can* anyone else be?

I've said it in a previous chapter, but it's worth repeating -- Do you really expect someone else to understand where you or your company is going when you don't? You may superficially believe you know where you are going, but do you really? In the long term – not just two, three or even five years, but for a lifetime – do you have an idea where you want to be and what kind of life you want to live?

Let me share a personal example that may help you get a better picture of what I mean. There came a time in my IT business where I really didn't identify well with it. Besides all the typical issues of dealing with clients, staff and issues that came up, I really didn't like what we were doing anymore.

It just wasn't enough to go out and fix computer and network problems anymore. I didn't enjoy getting up every day and doing the same old thing. I started to look at what we were doing as a whole and found myself measuring our value in the marketplace.

At first glance all appeared well. We were profitable, we had many happy clients and we had staff members who had been there for years. I wondered if it was just me that was dissatisfied. Perhaps it was just a sign of me burning myself out with all the hours I was putting in, often spanning into every weekend. In time, though, I realized that we were just going about our day like so many other companies, and their business owners and executives.

Suddenly something got a hold of me and I thought that perhaps it was time for me to head off in a new direction and that it was okay to do something new, something which I might find more fulfilling. After all, life is about experiencing things. Who said I needed to keep doing what I was doing, even though it was successful?

Of course this got the attention of all those around me, who were questioning why I would not stick with something I had learned and mastered in the past almost 20 years. Here too I just politely thanked people for their concern and decided it was time to plan my exit strategy.

When I did this, I started looking at my company in a whole new way. I started by reconstructing the organizational chart and developing each role with an eye on how the company can function without my involvement. During this process I redeveloped the passion for what I really enjoyed doing – this being the development of a business.

I also realized that it really had nothing to do with the IT business, it really was about the creative process, the challenge to do something that most people would never bother doing. This is also when I really got to understand what I was really meant to do and became tuned into my core strengths and talents. I remembered all the comments I had heard in the past, including those that said "why re-create the wheel?" I could just copy someone else's business model and do what most in our industry do.

Funny enough, this came from previous staff that felt my business development strategies took revenue away from their own pockets. All this helped me fully ground myself in what really was important to me and what gave me the energy to get up every morning excited about my day.

The Clearing Vision

The vision that came from all this was that I knew that I had a little more work to do before I headed off in some other direction, a vision that involved helping others. I wanted to share what I had learned, and to help them shave off some time and get to their goals faster than I did, hopefully with less pain. What I wanted to share went far beyond that of building a business. It was more about rediscovering life and using a business, or even a job, as a tool instead of an anchor holding you back and taking the fun out of life.

Using the example of my IT company, the vision I developed from the process of self-reflection was that I wanted to create an IT company that was much different than the average business that existed in the marketplace. I believed that the IT industry could use an overhaul. In my opinion everyone's "brother-in-law" claims to know about computers when, in reality, most people don't have a fundamental understanding of origins of computer technology as well as how everything goes together. I often refer to this as the *big picture*. What's worse is by missing the bigger picture and with increasing gaps in the way technology is often implemented and maintained over time, organizations are subjected to completely unnecessary business risks that their owners or investors are usually not even aware of. There's just not enough time spent on keeping an eye on what's most important.

Another component of my clearing vision was the development of a concept that I named "Peace of Mind IT". This concept would allow us to clearly define a set of systems and processes that, if used, would deliver the end result of "peace of mind" in-and-around technology. In the IT industry some of the most common gaps are found in the inability to recover data in the event of a major system crash; overall strategy in business continuity; and data and network security. The other gap we have found often lies within the leadership of a company.

In summary, we felt that far too often organizations are exposed to unnecessary risk - risk that causes service disruption within the organization, resulting in uncontrolled costs, frustrated employees, frustrated customers and sometimes even damage to the reputation of an organization.

In fact, it was these visions that evolved into other ideas such as the creation of a community-based website where the IT company that was to evolve would share the mindset, perspective, philosophy and lessons learned to those organizations that find value in the information being provided.

It turns out that this idea has added a whole new dimension to our organization. The idea is to give everyone involved an opportunity to contribute and feel part of something bigger - something that has purpose within what would normally be considered just a job. It would add value to our culture, we would have fun and everyone would get to experience how their contribution adds value to others – a value that seems to have been lost in our busy and often self-serving culture.

I moved from what was a really competitive marketplace (that of fixing computer network problems) to a company that would play a much bigger role in the marketplace and the communities it serves, and in a sense has virtually no competition. It isn't competition I worry about or even spend a lot of time on. It is how we can use our area of expertise to best solve real world problems.

The type of companies I resonate with are companies that continue to evolve over time, that never stop growing, embrace change and actively seek to enrich the communities they serve. Companies that are "in it" for more than *just making money* and have a sense of social responsibility. This goes far beyond a nice plaque on the wall or a clever mission statement. We are achieving this goal through a collaborative team effort utilizing both for-profit and non-profit models, and are dedicated to sharing our knowledge and experience with others.

What was the essence of that vision? To create a technology company that would place importance on the bigger picture. Recommendations and decisions would be based on facts, not hunches or guesses so often found in our industry. Through the course of our relationship with our clients, we would study each client's business, their specific needs and what makes their company work. This enabled us to help better align their technology to their actual business objectives.

Our IT company would place the highest value on our relationship with each client, and assure a meeting of minds - knowing that this would be key in our ability to align and deliver the kind of end result we would aim for.

In the area of technology where things change so much and so quickly, that if you don't keep your eye on the ball there, things get out of alignment very fast. Add to the fact that without IT systems most companies cannot exist and our job becomes extremely important and can have a major impact on an organization's growth.

We would develop ways to help those businesses grow and go beyond technology itself. Technology is supposed to serve people to be more effective in what they do. Often people need help in understanding its use and sometimes even its purpose, and they often require training that allows them to properly utilize the technology in their daily jobs.

A brief example of this is when problems develop within organizations because employees often feel the companies they work for are trying to control their use by restricting certain functions, especially in the social networking area. We often found ourselves helping employees understand the balance between productivity and all the security threats that can challenge the existence of their jobs and the financial stability of the companies they work for.

In order to deliver the bigger picture and be able to make the right recommendations we would need to engage at a much higher level than the average IT company would ever be able to do. In order to accomplish this we would only engage with clients that are willing to form a partnership that would enable us to put the right amount of resources on the job.

This partnership would not differ much from internal staff, require a monthly commitment that would allow us the ability to align our resources and processes in such a way that we would be able to deliver a specific and predictable end-result over time. Our client would have limited financial risk due to a fixed fee structure aimed at removing the adversarial relationship most commonly found in our industry where the technician typically gets paid over and over again – often fixing the same issue.

Our resources and systems would be designed to bring in more value than anyone they can have on staff as it takes about four different roles and a lot of specialized tools that would cost a company much more to own, implement and maintain themselves.

My vision as outlined above helps create a competitive edge as over 90 percent of IT competitors would have a tough time competing due to inadequacies in, or the absence of systems and processes, as well as insufficiently defined roles and responsibilities, etc.

In the end we had transformed into a company that:

• took initiative to make a much needed change in the marketplace

• put back the value in people

• knows who we are, has focus, and is selective to partner only with those organizations where we are successful in establishing a "meeting of the minds"

• keeps an eye on social responsibility

This had to be a two-way street, because part of that vision was to give our employees a great work atmosphere where they could challenge themselves to grow, both personally and professionally. They would be conduits of that vision in the marketplace and have a positive impact on the businesses we serve.

Of course, situations change. With a lifetime plan you have to adapt, overcome and improvise at times. But with a goal in mind, you can fill your day with actions that take you in the right direction, even if it's not the exact route you originally planned. Given a choice, would you engage in any activity that you were not absolutely clear is in the right direction? Typically when setting goals, people will say things like "I want to make a lot of money," or "I want to grow this business, and hire more people." There are many variations of these goals, but you get the general idea. Such goals often ignore the most important ingredient. How does this goal (or *these goals*) affect your life? If you reach your goal, how will it improve the quality of your life?

Answering these questions is important, because you can spend your life chasing goals, and even hitting goals, and still feel empty when you're finished. I know, because I did it myself. You feel this emptiness because you were never really clear about what you wanted out of your business and out of your life, and why.

Outside of the obvious perks and benefits – making a lot of money, driving nice cars, living in a nice house – what do you feel is your *mission* in your business? It's helpful to start with the end result you want in your life, and work your way backward.

For example, if you realize that your family is most important to you, then you know that you *don't* want a career that would always require long hours at the office. Of course every project or endeavor can occasionally take up a lot of your time. Could you find a career or business situation where you can spend time with your family?

This is a simplified example, but you see how setting priorities and establishing what's important to you – the end result – can determine the route you follow and the actions you take. Perhaps your mission is to build a business that provides personalized service to its customers. You pride yourself on the quality of your work and the attention to detail you provide.

When a giant mega corporation offers you a lot of money to buy you out, would you take it? You can take the money and run, or you can ignore the money and continue to provide service. Or, to put it another way, you can take the money and use it to provide personalized service in another way, while the buyers benefit from your reputation and learn from your experience.

How you decide such questions is based on your self analysis and deciding what's important to you. As discussed earlier, it is perfectly acceptable to build a mega corporation as long as it is something you are passionate about. It can be immensely rewarding both personally and financially. Don't let anyone tell you different, especially those jealous of you. When you do what is important to you, it really doesn't matter what other people think.

Some people want to build mega corporations, others are happy with a little store downtown.

What's important is that it serves you and your family in a way that you have a balance of all life has to offer. Always remember to notice if you are excited about your every day. It will tell you a lot, and please don't be discouraged if that changes over the years. It usually means it's just time to make an adjustment.

Life is about living, not being stuck doing the same thing every day. Just look at children and watch them play. They are creative, they are silly, they are living and engaged in life. Personally I think we need to go back to that place more often as the seriousness of life often gets the best of us.

Tools

Communication skills. Earlier I referred to communication skills as a vital part of what every person, especially someone in business, should develop. I mentioned *ambiguous messages, not accounting for noise* and *failing to listen.*

Ambiguous messages. If you're not clear on what you want to say, then how do you even know what to say? I've noticed that often people will say something, but then qualify it with remarks that invalidate the point they were making. It's like telling someone something, and then saying, "Not really."

Clarity of purpose is not only for the big questions in your life. It's for any time that you are communicating with someone, whether orally or with written language. You should be clear on exactly what you are trying to accomplish with your communication, and then use the proper form to accomplish that goal.

Not accounting for noise. In communication, noise is anything that interferes with the message you are trying to convey. If you are communicating with someone, you might forget that other people are also communicating with them. Have you ever been in a conversation with someone and their cell phone rings? Almost everyone answers their cell phone at such a time. You know how frustrating it is when you are trying to make a point and the other person turns his attention away from you to start a new conversation with someone else.

The same thing can happen in a number of different ways. If you are trying to give a new client a good impression, have you dressing professionally? If you wear blue jeans and a T-shirt to a meeting, then your clothes could present "noise" that interfere with the message you might be trying to convey.

Most industries don't consider such attire "professional." It is important to consider your environment and dress accordingly. Doing a little bit of research is worth a ton of gold and it will show up in the results you achieve.

You have to be aware of the danger of noise interference when you try to communicate. Identify it, account for it, and overcome it.

Failure to listen. One of the most important communication skills that you can develop is the ability to listen. Often the information you need is available to you if you will only pay attention to what other people are saying or writing.

E-mail, a Modern Form of Communication.

The problem with today's modern communication using emails is that they are very impersonal and so often the message is misunderstood and can easily offend the person reading it. Why? It is often misread because of the lack of the human interaction, being able to hear that person's voice, or seeing their bodily expression. It also does not provide the opportunity for the receiving party to interject.

Really think twice about this form of communication for anything that is really important and not just passing along information. This is an example of how technology doesn't always serve us if used in place of personal conversations. Sometimes you should be in front of that person, even though the conversation may be uncomfortable at times.

Far too often I see people using e-mail because they don't want to face another person. Although it is a way to get a message across without having to face the emotional aspects, often it causes more problems than if the situation were faced right there and then.

Most people are extremely poor listeners. They are engaged in the most very basic level of listening. They may hear the words the other person says, but they don't listen for understanding. They are simply waiting for the chance to respond.

Have you ever caught your attention wandering when someone else was speaking to you? This happens because instead of paying attention to the other person, our focus is on ourselves. We are so in love with the sound of our own voice, and so focused on what we're going to say next, that we often miss what the other person is trying to communicate.

Most of the time, if we give any indication that we're listening, it's with the nod of our head and saying "uh huh" at what we consider the appropriate times. Inside, however, we are telling ourselves:

- *I had an experience just like that*
- *This is starting to bore me*
- *I'm scared I will say the wrong thing and look stupid*
- *I have my own opinion on this one*

When we listen at this level, we are unaware of the other person and unaware of our impact on that person. We don't realize that our own results and effectiveness with people are skewed because of this.

Often the person you are listening to feels your silent messages intuitively, perhaps not able to put their finger on it. Your ability to influence them is greatly diminished as well as their ultimate respect of you.

Much more beneficial is *listening with attention*. At this level, your attention is focused sharply on the other person. Your listening is directed at the person speaking. You listen closely to:

- Words
- Expressions
- Emotions
- Values

It is essential to listen for what they *don't* say as well, and what energizes them. When you ask questions, do they come alive? Or do they become withdrawn? Are you watching their body language, the twinkle in their eye? Are you really connecting with this person? If this is hard for you then please practice.

There are great books and classes available on this subject. Practice the art of active listening; where you are repeating back to the person parts of what you have heard, showing them you are both interested and listening to what they have to say. It will also guide you in really understanding their message.

At this level we are listening holistically, regarding their words in context with the situation, their experiences, and the purpose for the conversation. The message that they are communicating takes place on many levels besides simply the words they use.

At the highest level of listening, you take in everything. You identify with the energy between you and the speaker. Although you are aware of what is happening around you, it doesn't distract you from the other person's message.

Your attention includes everything – what you see, what you hear, what you smell, what you feel.

At this level you readily detect shifts in mood or attitude. You have greater access to your intuition, so that the person speaking can almost speak in shorthand. Single words or phrases describe entire situations and circumstances. Moreover, you become intensely aware of your impact on the person speaking.

In the end, always remember that people want to be listened to. The person who understands that and makes a conscious effort to learn and enhance their listening skills will notice a tremendous power to influence the world around him or her.

Learning from others. Each of us lives a fairly short time, in a fairly narrow way. Even people who explore the world and meet many other people still have only what reaches their senses during any period of time. Personal experience, while valuable in learning, is still limited.

You can maximize your education by learning from the experiences of others. Find people who have been where you want to go and learn from them. Read their books, listen to their tapes, engage them in conversation. Find out what they went through to get there and improve on their experience. Do more of what they did right, and avoid the mistakes that they made.

One of my intentions with this book is for others to learn by what I've gone through. I have learned so much from listening and learning from others, taking their feedback in (although hard at times), and learning from them. Through this I know I have become a better and more fulfilled person.

You will find that people who have made it to great places and who stay there over time have a history of learning from others. They have learned that this is a never ending process of personal and professional growth.

You truly need to be engaged in the learning process from time to time in order to be an effective leader. A leader who thinks they have nothing left to learn is not the kind of person you should be taking a whole lot of advice from, as their personal and professional success is limited over time.

Personal Growth, Professional Growth and Leadership

I have a friend who I met through business, who I would call a *rainmaker* – someone who is really engaged in the selling process and who is very successful at it. He is keenly aware of the value that he provides to the customer. He also leads a sales team.

As this friend progressed in his career, he experienced some of the frustrations that go along with it. He's an intelligent guy, so he did a smart thing. He found a mentor to help in the area of professional development. During the time that he worked with this mentor he got a lot out of the arrangement.

One day, however, he told me that he was becoming a little frustrated. "I'm trying to learn about business, how to get better results and the like, but he keeps talking about my personal life." He was growing frustrated because he was paying this mentor for one thing and getting something else.

As I said, my friend is intelligent, so he knew the truth – that there comes a point where further *professional* development doesn't happen without some *personal* development first. That's hard for a lot of people, because it means that you are faced with opening up, confronting things that you have covered up your whole life. This is where the challenge lies and is essentially a form of fierce fear.

The good news is that if you keep an open mind, and work through the personal discomfort you experience when looking inside – and trust me, there would be times when you wonder why you are going through all of this – you will find yourself propelled forward in every area of your life.

Inspiring Others

When you find yourself in alignment with your purpose, and you do more of what you love every day, you discover that is when you have the most influence on the people around you. Your enthusiasm is literally contagious. People like being around you. They come from all directions to share your passion for what you are doing.

With clarity of purpose, passion for what you are doing, and the involvement of others in your mission, good things start to happen to you. You achieve results beyond what you thought possible. It seems inexplicable at first, unbelievable.

I call this the *inside to outside* approach. It all begins with you, with the image you hold of yourself, and your attitude about everything you do. Your internal work manifests itself externally, achieving results and attracting other people. It literally radiates from you. It's at these moments that you have the greatest ability to inspire others. This is true power and if used with sincere care and to the benefit of others it will take you on your road to fulfillment.

The funny thing is that achieving fantastic results and accomplishing more isn't even difficult when you operate at this level. Success seems to come naturally, springing from the circumstances in which you have placed yourself. There's nothing you need to learn, no special "technique" that you have to use.

When you haven't done the proper internal work, when you try to "fake it," then all the tricks and techniques in the world don't necessarily make things easier. Everything is an effort, as you use up all your energy keeping up a front, projecting a "happy face" to everyone around you, presenting prepared speeches.

All of your efforts are far less effective than if you had simply done the proper preparation beforehand.

The normal frustrations that usually drain you – handling angry and frustrated clients, disgruntled employees, arguments with those close to you – create far less friction. For anyone who hasn't experienced this, it may seem hard to believe. I can say for myself and in my own life that working from the inside first has changed my world significantly. I enjoy improving with every day.

The best part of dealing with your business in this way is that it spills over to your personal life. You will enjoy better relationships with: your significant other, your family, your kids, your friends, and everyone else whom you associate with. It truly enriches your life.

Thus, a great leader is someone who can be who he is as a person in every situation. He can be the same person at work, at home, or anywhere else and not have to put on an act within a specific role.

Just think of how easy life can be when you are so aligned that you know who you are, what your purpose in life is, what fulfills you, and have learned the skills necessary to properly communicate with others around you.

Encouraging Your Team

For anyone in business, there exists an enormous payoff for truly trying to understand the people around you. When you honestly get to know them, what excites them and gets them out of bed in the morning, you establish a connection that is tremendously productive.

Find out what the people around you look forward to. What do they do after work? On the weekend? What do they do and where do they go for vacation?

These non-work times are what they choose to do when they are not being paid – one of the most valid indicators of what excites them.

Don't assume that people know what it is that excites them. Most people aren't really that aware. As a leader in business you have the opportunity to help uncover those attributes and can help others lead more fulfilling and productive lives.

You will have an impact on their positions and help them gain the skills necessary to move into other areas both inside and outside your company's walls.

This will add fulfillment to yourself, those you put in charge of leadership as you grow and have a positive impact on your company. Don't underestimate the power of a company – your company – if your entire team is more fulfilled in their daily lives.

This is a prime example of how such a company can radiate a positive energy to the product and/or service it offers to the world around them. It will be a successful company! It's the kind of company I am building! Will you be joining me?

When you know these types of details about your team, it becomes easier for you to paint a picture of how what they do for you gets them more of what *they* want.

Allowing your team to see how every new proposal, every new project, every new assignment can also get them one step further toward their own goals, can help lift their excitement and enthusiasm in their work.

Remember, it isn't what you *think* you know about other people and what they want out of life; it's what they tell you with their words and actions.

This is where employing your listening skills effectively can do the most good for you and for them. You only obtain accurate information when you pay attention and get to know them as people.

The rewards for such an approach are tremendous as outlined in this chapter.

Great leaders know this. They inspire others by putting themselves in the other person's shoes.

With every single person who you deal with in your business or in achieving your dream, think of them as individuals with their own hopes and dreams. Find a way to help them get what they want by working with you.

Your task will be to help them clarify their own goals, what they truly want out of life. Just as you went through the process of self analysis and introspection – and may have found it difficult to do at times – they also face the same challenges. Be a coach. The typical person is unclear about how to go about reaching their own goals, or even how to properly define them.

Ultimately, your success – and not just financially – comes from how many people you encourage and inspire. You urge them to go after their own dreams, and you show them how to get there.

CHAPTER FIVE

The Benefits of a Clear and Strategic Vision

I wish that I were able to say that everything I've ever done has been perfect, and that establishing my career and my own company was smooth and without problems.

Of course, that wouldn't be true at all. I started out with a good idea, good intentions and with what I thought was a good vision. What I found out was that what I had in mind needed adjustment along the way, and a whole lot of attention in many different ways, some of which I didn't really understand at the time. Like many entrepreneurs or other ambitious people, I was busy and I didn't have time to take a look at my world and align my actions with my vision.

What is "vision?" Vision is a vivid description of what you want to create in the future. For an individual, a vision might be to become an astronaut, a teacher or a successful business person. For an organization, it might mean becoming the premier producer of a product or provider of a service within an industry.

The key word in the definition above is vivid. What you see for yourself or your organization should be completely clear. You should be able to taste, touch and smell it. This helps to get as much sensory detail in your mind as you possibly can. The more real that you can make the image, the better chance you have of realizing it.

What happens when we involve the brain and the imagination to such a great degree is that we are better able to achieve making the image a reality. It's like shooting an arrow at a target. The bull's-eye is easier to hit when you know and believe where it is and are determined to hit it. All your efforts and energy can go to making sure you're pointed in the right direction.

Some additional comments about your vision – it should be both *worthwhile* and *attainable*. It should be *worthwhile* in the sense that it is in alignment with your personal beliefs and values, and that it will benefit society. By this, I mean that a vision which depends on hurting or taking advantage of other people for its fulfillment is not worthy. The world will be a better place if you pursue and achieve a worthwhile vision.

Your vision should also reflect an advancement or improvement to your current situation. A "vision" that simply maintains the status quo is not really a vision. There are many aspects to improving your situation via realization of your vision, which I will get into later.

A vision should also be *attainable* – that is, something that can be achieved through your own efforts. You may not know the direct path, but what you picture in your mind is the culmination of your efforts and energies. It is the item toward which you focus yourself, and by the power of that focus you make it a reality. If the thing that you have in mind is not realistically something that can be done through your efforts, it's more dream than vision.

Like most people starting their own business, I did not begin with a true vision in mind. When I first began as co-founder of our quality management consulting firm in Germany and in working with larger companies, I saw the chaos that reigned throughout their organization. I was shocked that companies with a worldwide presence could have so many problems, problems that were often the result of the lack of a good vision.

When I started my own IT business, I stayed so busy with marketing, and then doing the best job possible helping customers with their computer problems, that any small vision I might have had at the beginning got swept away simply by how busy I was. Then – just like the larger companies I had seen with problems – I ran into all sorts of difficulties. There were difficulties in achieving the growth for the company that I desired, problems in achieving a consistent level of customer service, and a lack of commitment and communication among the members of my team. I knew I had to do something.

What I learned the hard way were a couple of things that a vision is *not*. It's not just a good idea. The business I started stayed busy, and we were extremely profitable. We had plenty of customers. The idea of the business itself was a good one – we were in the right place at the right time, doing the right things.

An enterprise based only on a good idea, however, is built on a shaky foundation. Unless the organization is very lucky, problems will start to arise because of the lack of vision. In my case, I was working long hours, and doing many of the less important tasks myself, simply because I felt I was better able to do them than anyone else. A long time employee quit on less than great terms, and I felt betrayed by his actions. I began to feel burnt out and used up. This was not at all what I had in mind when I started.

A vision is also not simply a matter of having good intentions. My customers were being provided with good service, and my employees were well paid and I was making good money. By most standards the company was successful, yet there was clearly something lacking. The issues that kept coming up seemed like things that could have been prevented if I had only planned better – in other words, if I had a really clear vision.

The Importance of Vision

A vision is a magical thing. It connects the present to the future. When you imagine something that you can achieve and create, you are looking ahead at the "what *could be*" rather than looking down at the "what is, now." You give yourself (or your organization) something to strive for.

This creation of an image that you are trying to make reality can sustain an entire company, because it gives everyone a sense of purpose. Instead of simply clocking in, putting in their day's work, and clocking out, people with a sense of the company's vision are invigorated. They are part of something bigger than themselves.

This ability to look ahead at what is being created prevents the "crisis of the day" mentality that many organizations suffer from. Rather than being caught up in the trap in which every challenge is a problem, and that each day is a never-ending stream of trouble, people who have a sense of the company's vision understand that overcoming challenges is simply part of the process of creating the vision.

The organization with a vision enjoys many benefits. For one thing, a company with a strong vision attracts commitment from its people. There is an excitement and an enjoyment when you're part of a creative team, working toward a common goal. Such an environment attracts and retains good people. Loyalty to the vision keeps them motivated.

A culture working with a vision in mind also energizes people. As I mentioned earlier, challenges are not roadblocks, but simply part of the process of realizing the vision. Team members are willing to go the extra mile when necessary. They also feel comfortable coming up with creative solutions, rather than waiting on others.

When an organization has a true, clear vision, it creates a standard of excellence for everyone to live up to. Without being told, team members understand that shoddy work is not acceptable when the vision is one of greatness. They know that they are expected to live up to a higher standard.

Strategic Vision

When you have the initial vision in place, it's time to implement what I like to call "strategic vision." Strategic vision is the systematic implementation of the larger vision. It's setting up systems, procedures and policies that help communicate the original vision to the members of the team. It's getting everyone's "buy-in" to the vision.

In my own case I had to find out the hard way that something was lacking in my own strategic vision. I once had a mentor who told me that life kind of has a way of tapping you on the shoulder from time to time, trying to get your attention. If you don't respond, then life comes back with a slap in the face. If that didn't work, then eventually a truck comes at you from nowhere and knocks you down. I have to admit that's pretty much what happened to me. Now I try to pay attention to the signs that I'm getting.

In my case, one striking example was in the area of sales and marketing. When I was just starting out, I did all the sales calls myself. My company provided extraordinary IT help, and my sincerity and belief in the company were apparent. When customers see that kind of commitment and dedication on the part of the salesperson, sales tend to go well, and I was very successful. As the company grew, it became necessary for me to hire other salespeople. I did everything I could to communicate my vision to the sales staff, but often it simply didn't work out. We set up plans, set goals, campaigns, etc., but things never really seemed to come together. Many times it was clear that they were working for a paycheck, rather than to share the company's vision with potential customers.

There were always excuses, of course. The market was not right, they didn't have enough time, they could do better with other sales techniques or materials – the list goes on and on.

One day I realized that the key was really inside me. The marketing people I had were seasoned professionals, and they had spent time with me learning why certain things worked for me, how I got started, the company history, and so on. What I had failed to communicate to them, though, was my vision for the company, and how it could benefit customers. In that sense, I had failed at implementing a strategic vision that would get the buy-in from my team.

Strategic vision helps everyone understand why the organization exists. This should not be a secret to anyone who is involved with the organization at all. The entire company, from CEO to the administrative staff, along with customers, potential customers and competitors, should have no doubt about what the organization exists for.

Every organization has core beliefs and values. A strategic vision ensures that these beliefs and values permeate every aspect of the company. Team members should understand what behavior is or is not acceptable when they are acting on behalf of the company. When faced with a decision between two priorities, they should be able to decide relatively quickly which one is more important, based on the values of the organization.

The difference between vision and strategic vision is subtle but distinct. The vision is the extra-clear image of something that exists in the future. Strategic vision is the establishment of conditions that can help to make the vision a reality. It adds to vision.

When strategic vision is implemented, it often involves the creation of systems to help make the vision real. Sometimes this involves a standardization of procedure, so as to ensure that the highest quality of product or service is more achievable. This goes back to what I said earlier about creating a standard of excellence. Human beings are prone to seek the easiest, fastest, most convenient way of doing something. Often the end result is a less than perfect result. By creating a systematic way of achieving goals, and a certain degree of standardization, the standard of excellence is maintained.

Some people object to "systems," because they think that approach stifles creativity. The opposite is more accurate – by showing people what the standard is, and how it can be achieved, they have the ability to apply their creativity and imagination to the system to make it better. They don't have to waste as much time on things that don't work.

Such an approach makes it possible for team members to achieve maximum results (in realizing the vision of the organization) in a repeatable way. This is often called a "best practice."

What happens is that newer people can learn from the experiences of veterans without having to go through the pain and take the time that the lesson originally took. It's the cumulative wisdom of the team. It's what ensures a quality standard in a product or service.

Implementing a strategic vision helps keep the organization closer to the original vision. Every single day, every single member of the team has forces pushing and pulling at them, affecting their decisions and the way they do things. The more people you have in your organization, the more forces there are. Each of those forces has the ability to distract someone from the organization's vision.

Strategic vision combats those distractions by providing a stabilizing force. Like gravity, it keeps everyone grounded so that they know what to expect and what is expected from them.

When asked to do something that violates the organization's values, they know it immediately and can respond appropriately.

When strategic vision is implemented properly, it simplifies every aspect of the company's business. Marketing is simpler, problem-solving is easier – everything becomes simpler because of the clarity that the vision brings to the organization. This is not to say that every problem is simple to resolve, or that problems disappear – but everything seems to click better.

Passion

The "tap on the shoulder" I received was within myself. Initially, when I first started my company, I was full of desire and energy. Everything seemed clear to me, and my enthusiasm carried the entire company with it. The company was very successful and we grew.

Even though I was successful financially, a few years after I started I found myself thinking more and more often of getting out of the company I had started. The long hours, the personnel problems that seemed to keep cropping up, the general lack of cohesiveness in the company, had worn me down. I had lost my *passion*.

Passion for what you are doing is an absolute requirement for success. You have to have that burning desire to create something, to achieve something that is bigger than yourself. When you have that burning desire you don't think about your days off or what you're going to have for lunch or any of the other distractions that can take away from your mission. You are absolutely focused on your goals.

That burning desire is what makes a person able to work long hours, do hard labor, and do unpleasant tasks that others won't do. Just as a car's engine is what drives it, passion is what drives people to commit themselves to doing whatever is necessary to be successful. More than simply motivation, passion seems to add fuel to a person's tank, making them able to do more than they might be able to otherwise.

When I started out, I had a clear understanding of my vision. I knew what I wanted to accomplish. That added to my passion, giving me energy. I was like most other entrepreneurs in that respect. When you're first starting out to go somewhere, it's easy to keep your destination in mind. Passion keeps your vision in the forefront of your thoughts.

As such, passion makes it impossible to focus on the negatives. Every road has its bumps, and if a person has passion those bumps are simply driven over. When you are looking ahead, you don't let tiny variances distract you. That's the benefit of passion – you keep your eyes on the prize.

Passion also compels everyone involved to strive for excellence. Anyone who is passionate about something – whether it's business, their music, their favorite sports team – refuses to settle for less than their best efforts. Enthusiastic and passionate team members are able to achieve much more, both in quality and quantity, than unenthusiastic, passionless teams.

Passion has a way of being communicated from one person to another. We are always attracted to someone who is passionate about a particular subject. There is something innate about us that another person's enthusiasm, energy and drive for a subject make them attractive to us.

Have you ever seen a speaker on a topic that was absolutely *in love* with his subject matter? The speaker's voice gets louder and you can just feel the connection with the topic being presented. Even the most mundane topics can become interesting when we are able to see it from that person's point of view. Experienced speakers know that the passion they bring to the presentation arouses the interest and involvement of the audience.

They know the value of passion.

There are many people in the world who don't really know what their passion is. They go through each day more or less on autopilot, with nothing arousing their enthusiasm. If you want to find your own passion, here are some ideas.

Do a gut check. Your body often knows things before your conscious mind does. Is there anything you do – anything *at all* – that makes you feel the best? Do you stand straighter, talk more confidently, feel lighter on your feet when doing certain things? Do you find yourself getting excited? Whatever it is, think about what aspects of the activity provoke the strongest response. That may be your passion talking to you.

Look around you. Are there aspects of your current job that interest you more than others? Often our passion is around a corner or behind a closed door. Look at all the different parts of your current position, your current duties, your department's role, and your company's mission to see if there is anything that makes you feel passionate about doing it.

Do you have hobbies? Sometimes this is the easiest way to discover your passion. You may have a hobby that provides you with an escape from the world. That's not what you're really looking for. What you want to do is look through your hobbies to see if any of them inspire you and make you want to achieve more. Look for the physical signs I described above to see if expanding your hobby into a business is what you need to do.

Often, as was my case, it's not a matter of finding your passion, but trying to figure out where you lost it. Especially for people who have worked hard pursuing a dream for a long time; the realization that you have lost your passion for what you're doing isn't always obvious. There are signs, though:

You're motivated by money. Money is many things – a sign of financial success, a unit of value exchange, something to be saved – but it shouldn't be the sole motivation for someone in their job. Of course we have to have money to survive, but there are plenty of ways to earn money. For your passion to be real, you should be working on something because you think it's worthwhile. You should retain the original vision.

Your performance is low. This is usually someone's first sign when they have lost their passion. No longer motivated by their vision, their enthusiasm and standards drop until the high performance that was so important to them earlier has dropped.

You're exhausted. There are times when a passionate person can be physically tired from their efforts. They usually find that a brief time off – anything from a good night's sleep to a week's vacation – is enough to recharge their batteries. What I'm talking about here is the emotional exhaustion that many people suffer from, where no amount of physical rest can restore them. As I said earlier, your body often knows things before your conscious mind does.

You constantly feel disappointed or frustrated. Occasional disappointments and frustrations are part of the human existence. No one has a perfect life where everything goes according to their expectations a hundred percent of the time.

However, when you feel that your life is absolutely *full* of frustration and disappointment, then it's clear that something is wrong. This mindset is often the result of the loss of passion for what you are doing. In this particular case, a cycle is established. Your lack of passion makes your efforts less effective, leading to lower results. The lower results cause frustration and disappointment, which in turn lessens your passion and the cycle continues.

So how do you get your passion back?

That's what I faced when I realized that where I was in my life was not where I had intended, and not where I wanted to be. It was a hard job, and it took some time, but I realized that I had to do certain things to get my passion back.

Think back. One of the first things I did was to think about what made me start my company in the first place. Obviously I wanted to make money and create a successful business. But that was not my initial motivation. Over the years working for others I had seen the frustration that people had when faced with computer problems. My original vision was to provide a service to such people so that they could have peace of mind.

It was thinking back to my original vision that prompted me to realign my company's efforts and actions. I emphasized that we were there to provide help to companies, but more important to lead them to a state of mind regarding their computers. It was not an easy transition, because many people had become accustomed to "the way things are" and resisted change. In time, though, the changes began to take hold.

I also realized that there were aspects of the job that I enjoyed more than others. I enjoyed working with software and information technology hands-on, but it wasn't what I liked doing the most. I liked motivating my team, drawing out the bigger picture and setting company goals, and helping our customers find solutions that solve their technology challenges.

I implemented changes so that I spent less time doing things I didn't really like, and I spent more time on priorities and in developing people.

Suddenly I realized that I was once again passionate about what I was doing. In my original vision I spent my time helping customers solve problems through my own efforts, but once the vision matured some, I knew that it was better to give them the peace of mind they sought by developing my team.

Where I had been trying to do everything myself before, I now involve my team in making the vision a reality.

It takes a lot of thought to create a true vision, one that can lead you to be more successful in your personal and professional lives. As I discovered, your original vision needs to mature some so that it more closely resembles the real thing you have in mind. I discovered that my original vision was too narrow, that a vision should fit a larger purpose of life. Instead of helping other people one by one, I discovered that developing a team to help others creates a much larger sphere of influence.

CHAPTER SIX

You Need Other People

We weren't meant to be on this earth by ourselves, even though often it may feel as though we are -- especially when you're trying to build a business. Whether you call them family, team members, stakeholders or partners, the important thing is that you recognize that you need other people. You need them for your own well-being and for the sake of your business.

When I co-founded my first business in Germany more than twenty years ago, I worked with partners. We were all fresh out of college and joined together to build a consulting company. Although we were all excited about building the company we had a lot of friction. The problems were caused by questions that should have been answered beforehand: who was in charge, who would run what part of the business, etc.

On the surface we had our roles and responsibilities defined, but there were areas of conflict and overlap that, at the time, didn't seem important.

Today I recognize how essential it is to have clearly defined roles and responsibilities. It is equally important to minimize the presence of larger egos. We also had some of those, especially straight out of school and armed for success.

When I moved to California and started my own company focusing on information systems I was successful, but as the business grew I needed help. My wife started handling various aspects of the business and we began to hire people. We started with hiring contractors, but eventually needed employees. Of course, with an expanded staff we had a new set of responsibilities to navigate through, ranging from labor laws, payroll, additional insurances, and various other personnel issues.

With each level of involvement from other people, there were challenges. Using contractors was easy and straightforward in some ways, but not in others. It didn't require a whole lot of financial commitment on my part because I didn't have to worry about paying them when I didn't have work for them.

This worked out pretty well at first, but ultimately it failed, because I couldn't get sole commitment from them to service my clients when I needed them serviced. The contractors would either not have time because they were busy on other projects or they just weren't ready to do the work when I needed it done. There was also a lack of commitment to the client, and to my business. The result was that service quality was not where it needed to be.

When you're in the business of solving computer problems for people – or any other service requiring urgency - the concept of *later* doesn't work well. For instance, when a computer is not running right the customer is unable to work. My customers were always about ten minutes away from looking through the yellow pages to find someone who would respond *now*.

I often found myself picking up the ball and taking care of the customer myself. Today, on the one hand, I realize that the problem was the poor job I did of communicating my expectations to the contractor, and, on the other hand, I recognize my inability to control their time. Ultimately the contractor model just didn't allow me to control the quality of service I desired to achieve in my business. What I needed were *employees.*

Having full-time or part time employees carries a whole new level of commitment. I remember clearly when I made the choice to hire full-time employees. It was nerve-wracking. I had tried a couple of different methods such as hiring a former contractor, using part-time employees, and a combination of these, that hadn't worked out. I knew I needed a committed full-time staff to help me service our customers.

My wife and I began interviewing and hired a full-time person. Four months later we hired another. Looking back, I realize what a risk it was for me to hire these people. Cash flow is always an issue in every company, and here I had added two extra salaries that needed to be paid. I didn't have a real plan at the time. I simply knew that I couldn't do it all myself. I also wanted the business to grow.

An interesting thing happened. I knew hiring employees and growing the business would work in theory and fortunately chose to put some faith into it. That year, even with the added costs of the extra salaries, my own income from the business actually increased. Working together we were able to do more work and generate more income. I was able to focus on bringing in new customers to an already working service model.

With this small group I was able to explain what I needed and what the company was all about. Having employees who were committed to the process and mission of the company, although in a very linear way, was heading in the right direction and generated measureable results. Everyone was doing their job and making money. In the following years we continued to grow as a company and also as individuals. The number of employees, compensation and our shared success grew in proportion to our income as a company and we continued to learn new lessons.

Over the years I've made my share of mistakes, but one thing that I have learned is that I have to make a commitment to my team for them to make a commitment to me or the business.

I spend a lot of time with the key people I hire. Yes, it takes a lot of time and energy that could be spent doing other things, but it can't be done from the outside. It truly is an inside job. This is especially true when building your key management team.

This team will help keep the company's vision alive and be able to translate the vision to others within the company. It all starts with you -- knowing who you are what you want and what you stand for, and being able to effectively express that to your team.

Hiring People and Treating Them Right

When it comes to hiring and developing people for my business, I have designed a process that helps me do a better job. There is work to do, but the effort will ultimately fulfill not only your personal goals and dreams, but that of your staff's and to all those around you.

Step #1: Hire right. I now take the time to more narrowly define who it is we're looking for. I ask myself a variety of questions to help me narrow down my candidates. Questions like:

- What type of personality is best suited for the job at hand?

- Does the job require a calm and laid back personality to deal with stressful situations?

- Would an energetic personality be more likely to engage others?

- Will the person interact with the staff, the customer or both?

- Does the person need to have good verbal and/or written communication skills?

- What specific skill sets are required for the particular position available?

Once in interview mode:

- First impressions. How do they present themselves? Did they make an effort to prepare themselves?

- Why did they respond to the job ad? Do they know what they want in a job or is it largely undefined?

- Is the candidate an optimist or does he or she lean more towards pessimism?

- Will they fit into our company culture, get along with others and be in sync with our philosophies?

- How is their track record with employment? Do they have large gaps? Do they have a pattern of taking time off, perhaps a lack of focus or commitment?

For positions outside of management I have found that it's almost easier to hire someone with less experience, or who is at a point in their life where they are not trying to control everything and everyone around them. We've found two categories in particular which have proven valuable to us.

The inexperienced person tends to be more enthusiastic, more eager to learn, has a sense of what goals they want to achieve and tend to be more willing to listen to instruction. Typically (but not always) younger and just starting out, the inexperienced person often requires training in some areas more than others. The advantage that I like is that there is less "unlearning" of bad habits. These people are often a blank slate on which I can imprint my company's way of doing things. I also like the thought that they will learn important skills that will help them further their careers and add quality to their lives. It's actually one of those core values I have built into our company -- I want to run the kind of company that embraces the opportunity to enrich people's lives that work for us and set them up for success within or outside of my company.

The more mature person has the benefit of lots of experience. They are often already trained in many aspects of the job. The right candidates are those who have reached the point where they want to work for our company for the right reasons -- they believe in the company's mission and seek fulfillment from their work. Such people tend to radiate positive energy, making them natural leaders. The right candidates also embrace change when it's needed. Often someone in this category can move into management in a shorter period of time.

In the end the most important factor is that you take time to hire the right person. You must take the time to properly evaluate whether they are the person that really fits what you have in mind. Choose someone whose values are in sync with your company's values and vision. To do this you must be completely clear about what it is you're looking for. If you don't have that kind of clarity today, one that you have taken the time to write down, then this would be a great place to start.

There are a variety of resources to help you find the right person, one of them being a job hunter. If you choose this route, you would be wise to sit down, grab a piece of paper and give some thought as to who would fit into your culture. What type of personality would get along with you, with other staff, your clients? You can use some of the example questions earlier in this chapter to get you started. If you haven't done so already, then take the time to define your own values, as well as your company's. It is extremely helpful in aligning expectations. It works wonders when you take the time to define these areas and it creates clarity.

When you are done and in preparation of a job posting, grab a second piece of paper and write up a paragraph or two with a brief description of your company, the position and the kind of person you are looking for.

Make a conscious effort to define your expectations. Doing this up front will aid greatly in finding someone that is best suited for the position. Hiring the wrong person is not only time consuming, but expensive. Once properly prepared, you can use your written outline as the basis for a job posting or to circulate to a job hunter.

If you go to the higher quality job hunters you will most definitely have options to have access to more advanced testing processes which, depending on the caliber of person you are looking for (especially management), would be a worthwhile investment.

There are multiple other resources that can test your top candidates for a fee. These resources also come in handy if you are hiring employees yourself and I would encourage you to get familiar with their advantages. As a minimum I would definitely recommend a background screening process on every employee you ever hire. It sets a good standard, saves you potential costly surprises and says a lot to your hard-earned customers.

Step #2: Develop a system. Developing a system is absolutely essential after you have the right people in place. It is a system which will make everything come together and ultimately give you the freedom you are looking for. It is also a system which will set your people up for success, as it will guide them through the process of how your business works and how things must be done in order to achieve its primary objective.

In short, a system is that which holds the processes and procedures that enable your company to achieve the result it is out to deliver in the marketplace. It contains the specific steps in a specific order to deliver very specific results. It defines your company's way of doing things. A well thought-out set of processes can be invaluable for a company trying to deliver a consistent level of quality in its service or product.

There are many types of systems within an organization: systems in operations, business development, finance, training of employees, etc.

Much of what I learned about developing systems was from my time consulting for other companies in and around quality management. I also learned even more while personally implementing a comprehensive quality management system in my own company spanning over many years.

I understood how preparing in advance can prevent problems later on. I have seen many businesses over the years that have major gaps, even a complete absence of systems. These businesses struggle and are destined to fail.

If you want your endeavor to succeed over the long haul then I encourage you to spend time developing and implementing appropriate systems. These systems will ultimately be the glue that holds your organization together as well as set up your employees to succeed. Developing systems takes time and an entire book can be written on this subject alone. However, even a simple set of checklists along with clear job/role definitions is a great start.

Step #3: Spend time with your staff. This was easier to do early on when I had a smaller staff. With a larger staff it's more difficult, but it's even more important to do it. As the number of employees grows so does the "distance" between them and the company's vision. For them to feel connected to the company and its mission, they need face time with the leaders of the company.

As you grow you will need to find ways to stay in contact with your staff on a bigger scale. Many of the most successful companies do this very well. In our company we are leveraging the media which can be as simple as a recorded set of messages from the company's leaders to the staff during initial training as well as on an ongoing basis.

How you do it is not as important as that you actually *do* it and make it part of your culture. You will never get the best out of your people if they don't feel that you care. To get the very best out of your employees you have to allow them to grow as people from a personal and professional standpoint.

You will need to think about how you can add value to their lives beyond money and things. You will need to develop a sense of compassion for all their personal issues and learn to steer them in the right direction. There will be times in their lives where they just don't have it all together. The sincere effort on your part and that of your management team in this area will create measurable results. It's all part of being a better leader, and the best part is that your customers will notice it too. Happier staff equals happier customers.

Step #4: Allow your staff to take responsibility. This leads to the concept of delegation, which is often hard for leaders to do. I know it was difficult for me. However, for people to grow as individuals they have to be given responsibility for things and be held accountable for the results. People rise to challenges, and it does them a disservice if they are never given a chance to see what they can do.

At the same time, giving people responsibility trains them in new roles. They become more capable, better trained, and gain a better perspective of how different parts of the organization work together. As they gain this perspective they will develop a deeper understanding of the roles of their co-workers and peers, as well as the relevance their role has within the organization.

Giving them responsibility also allows them to better see the negative effects when they fail to deliver their specific part. Armed with this perspective they are much more likely to perform at a greater level of excellence. They become more confident. With a staff full of such people, lead by a strong leadership team, the success of the organization is poised to grow.

Step #5: Hold your staff accountable. To give someone a responsibility and not hold them accountable for the results does not help you or your company and would require someone else to monitor all that this person does. Besides that, it really doesn't teach them anything. It is important that your staff answer for the results, good or bad.

When assigning responsibility and accountability, remember to also give them authority. They have to be able to do the job without constantly asking permission from someone else to do the steps required. When people have full ownership of a task or project they are better able to complete it successfully, and they are more motivated to succeed. If you're concerned about your staff "messing up," then develop simple routine processes that will serve as a type of audit. Audits like this are useful tools to catch problems and allow corrective action through additional training sessions.

Ultimately Accountable:

Although you will need to hold everyone accountable for their own results in the roles they serve, it is essential that only *one* person is accountable for a given end-result to be achieved. If this is left undefined you will find a lot of finger pointing in the process, creating a negative effect on team spirit.

Sample:

If you have a product to be manufactured, only one person will hold ultimate accountability that the quality of the product delivered to a client is up to par. If you are providing a form of service, only one person can ultimately be held accountable for successful delivery – like a project manager. Others may play a role, such as with the production of automobiles. One person is responsible for the successful assembly of an engine, but the successful delivery of an automobile is that of yet another person.

These details are all part of a quality management system and need to be documented and visible to all in the organization. Most important though is that everyone needs to understand that these roles and responsibilities are there to help keep the organization in tact. Mistakes made are to be openly exposed (not criticized) so that corrective measures can be made to better fulfill the organization's promise in a successful product or service delivery.

Step #6: Challenge your staff to grow personally.

When an individual grows, that person contributes to the wellbeing of the entire organization. It is the leadership of an organization that can have the most dramatic effect in the development of an individual. It is up to the leadership team (even if it is just you), to bring out the best in your employees. Your people spend a third of their day serving the purpose of your organization. Although most focus on *professional development*, it is essential that *personal development* is in direct proportion. A person must grow personally first in order to maximize themselves professionally.

An example of this theory is a promotion to a leadership position such as department manager. In order to be successful as a department manager it is essential that you have gained not only the technical skills of that position but are emotionally ready to deal with a staff member who may come to you challenged with a personal issue. Someone may seek professional advice when the root cause is a personal one. The manager must be able to *read* this in his people even though they may not be able to effectively communicate it.

At our technology company we always placed a high value on the personal development of our team. In fact, we continually built new ways to enhance the personal growth of each person and role by adding directly to our training programs. We adopted this as part of our philosophy and company culture and it has become an important part of the core values.

Step #7: Challenge your staff to grow professionally. In some companies, mine among them, the motto is "the learning never ends." Whatever the people in an organization learn, it adds to the cumulative knowledge of the group. Besides performing better each person becomes a reservoir of information for everyone else.

Professional growth also calls forth the leadership in your organization. Far too often people are misplaced, even promoted into positions they are not best suited for. Added to that, many people are not really aware of their own personal strengths and talents, which you can test by asking them to define those.

Often you will hear them respond with *subject knowledge* they have obtained instead of having defined their actual strengths and talents. You can usually get a good start in defining these when you get to know people on a personal basis and listen to what they do when they go home. You will hear things like crafting or building in and around their homes, communities, etc. You will hear people engaged in hobbies or community services that give them a sense of fulfillment. You will find people that write, problem solve, sing, play music, etc.

All these are indications of their strengths and/or skills. If you have a strong and mature leadership team within your company you will gain insight on these things and be able to help shape some of these abilities into roles within the workplace. As a result you will create the type of workforce that is inspired instead of simply punching the clock every day. Here too, it is one of those things your customer will also notice, because this kind of positive energy radiates outward.

Treating people right is another part of building a successful business. It's been said that you can be efficient with *things*, but you can't really be "efficient" with *people.* Howard Gardner, a professor of education at Harvard University, has identified several different types of "intelligence."

Interpersonal relationship skills are one of the specified areas of intelligence that Gardner singles out. Such intelligence is characterized by the sensitivity an individual has to other people - their moods, feeling, and motivations. You basically understand what people need to work well. It is in direct relationship with the quality of your relationship with others around you. Are you skilled at communicating with other people? Do people seem eager to confide in you, to take you into their confidence? Is it easy for you to empathize with others, to see their point of view? Are you charismatic, or a natural leader? Being able to work well with others, to collaborate on projects, can also indicate a high level of relationship skills.

This type of skill is invaluable to anyone wishing to build an enterprise which calls for the help of other people. One definition of success uses the quality of our relationships with other people as its measure - meaning you become like the people you surround yourself with. Few lives that don't involve other people can be regarded as successful. Many notable accomplishments and inventions that we assign to a single person depended on others to be accomplished. Sir Edmund Hillary, the first man to climb to the peak of Mount Everest, was accompanied by Tenzing Norgay, a Sherpa guide. They also had a support team who had remained at a lower camp. Hillary's "individual" accomplishment was made possible because of his relationships with other people.

Human relationships are complex because each of us approaches every other person, and every interaction, based on our own perspectives, our view of the world. All of our prejudices, notions and beliefs come into play when dealing with other people. These different beliefs, affect everything that happens in the relationship, bouncing off one another like lasers bouncing off of mirrors. The multitude of possible interactions, multiplied by the huge number of consequences, create an incredibly complex system of relationship issues.

Many, if not most, people proceed through their days bumping into others in their relationships, occasionally aware that there are problems, but unaware and uninterested as to the causes of those problems. We are simply too busy as a society to give the proper attention to something which should be at the top of our priorities – the well-being of our relationships. The simple fact that we *are* so busy testifies to the importance of maximizing the valuable resources of other people.

For people to be on the same page with projects, with the company's mission, with almost anything in life, they first have to be aware of one another as individuals. A single bad relationship between two people can throw an entire project off. That's why it's so important for the leader to be aware of what's happening with his people, and to make sure he's doing everything he can with his own relationships.

In his book *The 7 Habits of Highly Effective People*, Stephen Covey discusses the concept of the *emotional bank account*. Like a regular bank account you make deposits and withdrawals, except instead of money you use emotions. If you help a friend move furniture, you are making a deposit. Make time to have a conversation with your daughter about something that's important to her and you make a deposit. Even with the strongest relationships, you can get your emotional bank account into the red.

If you ask a friend for a favor too many times, no matter how good the friendship is, he will eventually begin to feel that you are taking advantage of him. Go to a friend complaining about your life too many times, and he will begin to avoid having conversations with you. You are making too many withdrawals from the emotional bank account, and your account is overdrawn.

To strengthen relationships, focus on making deposits into a person's emotional bank account. Show kindnesses, both large and small, without being asked. Volunteer to help wherever you can.

If the question comes up about why you are being so thoughtful, tell them simply "I value our relationship, and I want to make sure that you know it."

Of course, this technique is also useful with relationships that may have deteriorated. However, if you start doing favors for someone when your relationship is on rocky ground, they may suspect you of ulterior motives or of being manipulative. In that case, what you consider *deposits*, the other person considers *withdrawals*. Trust must be established before deposits into the emotional bank account can be made.

Finally, look at establishing new relationships. Perhaps there are individuals who you classify as acquaintances and who you'd like to know better. If you already engage them in conversation, ask questions to find out their interests and concerns. Becoming genuinely interested in other people is the key to forming new relationships.

Always keep in mind the concept of making deposits into the emotional bank account. Deposits only count if they are of value to the other person, and you can only know that if you genuinely care about them.

If you look on having good relationships as a part of your purpose, then you can see how, despite temporary differences of opinion or viewpoints you might have with someone else, your focus is always on keeping the relationship strong and productive.

What constitutes a "strong and productive" relationship? It's one in which both parties benefit. For example, you would never want to approach someone to invest in your company if he was not going to earn a profit. You would merely be using that person for selfish personal reasons.

However, if you approach a potential partner to offer him a chance to invest, and in return you offer a solid chance at a good return on his money, then both of you benefit from the relationship. It would be productive.

If you approach a new relationship with only your own goals in mind, then it is doomed to fail. A productive relationship requires balance to survive and thrive. Of course, you have objectives that you want to accomplish, but they cannot be your primary motivation. Benefits to the other person have to be established early on for a relationship to take hold.

With a productive relationship, the interests of both parties are advanced. In the case of the business partner mentioned above, it was his financial well-being that was advanced. For others, it may be emotional well-being that is improved.

To improve another person's emotional well-being, you must be the type of person who fosters positive emotions. The other person in turn fosters your emotional well-being. In a productive relationship, whether financial or emotional, your interaction is *win-win*. Everyone benefits.

Such relationships are much more fulfilling when you share *core values* with the other person. Basic concepts like honesty, trust, respect and communication must be important to both of you. When you share values, then you hold similar outlooks on life. The bonds that connect you are strong.

This doesn't mean that you have to agree with every opinion

that the other person holds. People of integrity can hold different beliefs on any topic, even such hot button issues as politics or religion. When you share core values then those differences can be discussed without threatening the relationship. Differences can be acknowledged and respected.

In a fulfilling, productive relationship, the relationship itself takes primary importance. Differences can be discussed without either person feeling diminished or threatened. Of course, this can only happen when each party respects the other. Holding the individual in high regard is a key requirement for a strong relationship. When you have that kind of regard for someone, personal attacks are not even a consideration. The relationship takes priority.

When you have established boundaries that you both respect, then a relationship of this kind recharges and revitalizes you. When you agree on something, you feel better and both your interests are advanced. When you disagree – agreeably – then you are presented with a different viewpoint that may open your own mind to new possibilities. You advance because your vision and your options have expanded.

There is no chart or graph to determine when or under what circumstances you should keep or break a commitment with a friend. Every broken commitment is a withdrawal from the emotional bank account, and too many withdrawals can destroy trust. Honoring commitments both large and small, on the other hand, are huge deposits in the account, and a relationship will flourish with that kind of investment.

The main thing to remember in any relationship is that trust cannot be assumed automatically. It must be earned. The only way to earn trust is to honor the relationship and to follow the fundamental principles of honor and decency.

One of the things that I discovered through my experiences

over the years is that much of the jealousy, envy and destructive competitiveness I saw were because some people view life as a zero-sum game. In other words, if they saw someone else winning they believed that it meant that they themselves were "losing." What they lacked was the abundance mentality.

When it comes to abundance and money, things get really interesting. I call it people's *money programs*. Often so strong these money programs can become quite destructive. When a person worries or feels that someone is going to have a financial advantage over them, it can destroy business partnerships, friendships and families. I've seen it personally and within my own family. One common scenario is that of an inheritance, where people seem to come out of the woodwork fighting for their share. I've seen monetary disputes happen to other business owners to the demise of the companies they've built. Justified or not, it is the sheer focus on money and perceived "loss" or disadvantage that often becomes a hurdle in itself.

Skewed also is a person's mindset for making money to support their daily lifestyle. People don't realize that focusing on *money* with such intensity just creates more intensity in and around the subject of money itself. Instead of focusing on the problem of *not enough money or how am I going to pay for something I want to have* – I like to focus on what I can do to *earn* it. That is why I refer to a phrase I often use, "*You will always get paid in direct proportion to the service you provide to others*".

Sad is when money becomes the barrier to wishing others success in their doings, especially when it comes to creating a successful business. Far too often the competitive natures of our fellow human counterparts don't support us in getting too far ahead of another – supporting the mindset of *scarcity* rather than that of *abundance*. Even sadder is that this same mindset is what gets in the way of personal abundance and why I like to say that *amateurs compete and professionals collaborate*.

The abundance mentality recognizes that the universe is limitless. There are plenty of riches, either material or spiritual, for everyone. Each person can have a piece of the pie, and if we look hard we can see that the pie gets bigger any time we achieve success that is in line with our worthy values.

This key concept is recognized by anyone who has achieved lasting success. Look at the number of billionaires who have started programs or foundations to help others. There is a balance in the universe that determines whether you are worthy of having the success you work so hard to attain. Those with the abundance mentality know that universal law can't be broken – you can only break yourself against it.

When everyone involved has this mentality, not only is the environment more productive, it's more fun. People who are working together to achieve something great enter each day with a joyous, sometimes laughing, demeanor. Even when obstacles present themselves and progress is harder to make, those with the abundance outlook know that they are not in the struggle alone and can enjoy the camaraderie and fellowship with their partners. Hard work shared and a difficult task completed brings people together in ways that are unknown to those who always want to take the easy way to success.

The abundance mentality is the opposite of the scarcity mentality (the zero-sum game, "if you win, I lose" philosophy.) Working with others to achieve a goal creates a synergy that makes the impossible possible. What those with an abundance mentality find is that sometimes the whole is greater than the sum of its parts – that is, a team can accomplish more working together than what each member could achieve on his own.

President John F. Kennedy once said, "The rising tide lifts all boats." Shared success benefits everyone and a higher level of success means greater success for all involved. This is why the loner who believes that he can only achieve his success by himself misses out on true success. By helping others achieve their own dreams and goals, you gain when they do - greater success and fulfillment than ever possible on your own.

This concept works off of the idea that all things in the universe are interrelated. The butterfly effect is a concept that small actions in one area cause great results in other areas. There may not be a direct line of causation between two events, but with the complex relationships in the world that have been scientifically demonstrated – changes in the environment, for example – there is no question that every action we take has repercussions of which we are unaware.

This idea goes beyond simple cause and effect. Especially in human interactions, we never know what small action we take has a profound effect on someone who we'll never meet. The world record for toppling dominoes was set in 2008 in The Netherlands. Organizers there set up a huge display of four and a half million dominoes that fell in sequence, creating beautiful patterns and effects. Do you think the first domino knew the last domino?

With all this discussion of relationships, I have hinted at something that I hope you have picked up on – integrity in dealing with others. Why is integrity important? Because it shows an adherence to values. Personal integrity leads to everything else – business integrity, organizational integrity and societal integrity. While you can't always count on others to display integrity, those around you should be able to count on *you* to display it.

Trust is built on a consistency of values. Ralph Waldo Emerson once said, "A foolish consistency is the hobgoblin of little minds." The key word here is *foolish.* Consistency of values does not mean sticking to worn-out ideas or concepts, or to techniques that have been shown not to work. Values such as honesty, caring and doing good work are not foolish in the least. Adhering to them means that others can count on you to do and act in certain ways. You demonstrate that you are trustworthy.

Consistency is the concept that underlies the American legal system. You may have heard the phrase that America is a "government of laws, not men."

This means that laws apply equally to all people, regardless of who they are. When someone enters a court of law, they count on the legal system to treat them in ways consistent with what has happened in other courts of law previously. That's why the Supreme Court relies so heavily on precedent, or on decisions that have gone before.

It's true that this concept has met with more or less adherence. A system, no matter how perfect, that is administered by human beings will eventually begin to reflect occasional human flaws. The ideal is still there, though – consistency builds trust in law and in personal relationships.

You may occasionally find yourself acting in ways that conflict with your values. As a human being, you will not always be perfect. When that happens, admit your error, correct it, and act in the proper way. If you've built trust with those around you, they will forgive you and the trust is not broken. That trust interaction is based on integrity.

Having a reputation for that type of integrity will expand beyond your immediate relationships. Integrity has become such a rare commodity in today's society that those who display it become known for it. News stories are written about people who return wallets with the money still in it.

When you have that type of reputation you attract others to you. Especially when it's heard from a third party, a reputation for honesty and integrity will attract other people that want to do business with you. ("Business" may have to do with commerce or simply friendly interaction.)

How do you go about developing and demonstrating such integrity? It's simple – *keep your promises on small things.* Keeping a promise, to yourself as well as to others, marks you as someone who can be trusted. I use the word "promise" here in a very flexible way.

Something as simple as keeping an appointment can be viewed as a promise. Keeping a promise simply means doing what you say you're going to do.

Of course, leading a life of keeping promises is tremendously difficult. If one of your values, however, is to keep your promises then decisions can become easier, even if their implementation is hard. For example, if you say you will meet someone for lunch and you have a flat tire, then keeping your promise means you lock your car and get to the restaurant at the appointed time. The easy way would be to call the person and say you can't make it – but that would be breaking your promise. As understandable as such a reaction would be, it is still a small breach of trust. Going the extra mile to fulfill such a promise marks you as a person of unusual integrity.

When you keep your word on such small things, then keeping your word on large things is much easier. It eventually becomes a habit, one which marks you as a person who can be trusted. Doing the right thing is almost never the easiest path to take, but it is the one that will attract other people to you and help ensure your success.

But, you might say, why is attracting other people to you so important? On the most fundamental level, it's because other people can help you. In an illogical way, though, you can't help others *because* you want them to help you. You have to help others (and thus attract them to you) with the spirit of simply being helpful. Keeping your word to them can't be simply to manipulate them into helping you. You have to live according to your values because that's the kind of person you are, and attracting other people – and their help in achieving your goal – is a byproduct of the person you are.

As I mentioned before, your efforts are multiplied when you are part of a team or partnership. You become part of a true team or partnership when you demonstrate those qualities that make you attractive to others. Your reputation for integrity will be the top calling card to attract other people to you and to your company.

CHAPTER SEVEN

What Are You Talking About?

In today's world, communication is king. We interact with so many different people on a daily basis that the potential damage from miscommunication is immense. By developing clear communication skills we can avoid problems and stand out in a positive way.

Clear communication and clear thinking go together. It's difficult to effectively communicate to another person when you aren't really clear yourself, or when you haven't taken enough time to clarify your own thoughts. I know it's often just easier to talk, to tell someone what you want to say and not to put much time and thought into it. After all, it's natural to believe that when you speak, people should listen. Unfortunately this way of thinking doesn't serve anyone well. Clear communication encompasses several different components.

Precision. Clear communication is the ability to deliver precise information on the subject at hand so that your audience can understand what it is you want from them. It is easier for everyone. To be precise, you have to provide essential information, and cut out all the rest that just convolutes the conversation to the point of confusion. It is usually then when people just can't follow anymore and they start missing things. It has been my experience that in order to cut out irrelevant information you really have to spend some time with yourself thinking about what exactly it is you want to achieve.

Brevity. This one takes practice and I don't claim to have mastered it, but I work hard at it every day. Especially since I have discovered how powerful a well communicated speech or set of instructions can be when it is precise and to the point. Typically words come out and I just blurt out my thoughts. What I've found, however, is that when I use one-third of my normal allocation of words, I have achieved the best results.

Relevance. Another important point to remember is that your communications really need to be relevant to the subject matter at hand. Think of your audience. Relevance goes hand in hand with everything else, and this is another reason to take some time to really think things through. Cut out things that just don't matter, that go off on a tangent and leave people wondering *what is this guy talking about?*

One way this used to show up for me was in my business while talking to clients or prospects. I used to think that I just like to talk and didn't give it much more thought. I had good results, but in time I got really frustrated that my meetings and discussions took so long. I was always running late to the next appointment or other things I needed or wanted to get done.

Of course I had feedback from co-workers and other people in my circles that felt I was going off topic too much and that I lost my audience. This was at first a bit too hard to take, so I didn't spend much time worrying about it.

However, over the years I have learned to realize that this really isn't serving me very well and that I was actually being disrespectful to others with these long winded conversations. I was robbing them of their valuable time. Perhaps it took me to start valuing my own time a bit more before making this connection.

Once I realized the value of time, I was almost embarrassed when I abused a conversation and so I started becoming more aware of it. Today, I still often have the urge to just keep talking and dive into every detail, but I remind myself that it just doesn't serve me, or the person I am talking to.

It takes some practice to master, but it is worthwhile to pursue. If you are looking for an outlet to practice being more precise in your communication and can see it is a valuable asset, you might want to consider participating in a public speaking seminar or your local Toastmaster Chapter. These types of resources can support you in mastering this technique simply because when you are faced with a 2-minute speech in trying to convey your message, you start to realize how valuable precise words effectively deliver a message. Also valuable is seeing how the wrong words leave everyone wondering what you are talking about after your 2-minutes are up.

My desire to master this skill in business also served me in my personal life and the relationship with my wife, kids and friends. It kind of just happened. All of a sudden I found myself getting more to the point and things just seemed to be smoother.

I realized that with this more precise and brevity-driven communication style, my conversations became more interesting for people and they paid better attention. My conversations were just that much more insightful and of value. This made me feel good about myself and I'm sure it is a relief to others.

Clear Thinking

Clear thinking is ultimately what drives clear communication. Before speaking, I like to remind myself of the following thought:

How can I communicate effectively when I am not clear about what I want? You have to know the *purpose* of the conversation if you want to communicate effectively.

I really do want to get my point across. It is just too frustrating when people don't get what I'm trying to say, especially when it costs me money. The energy required to redo things also causes stress. Repeating myself doesn't seem to get the result. In fact it sometimes makes the situation worse.

Most people don't want to be around someone who is getting frustrated. When you master the skill of knowing the purpose of a conversation, you really do get more of what you want. Who wants to get the wrong result?

This practice also goes for the other person. It just has to be a win-win for everyone. It isn't just a cliché, and especially this part needs to be taken seriously. It isn't worth trying to get someone to do something that isn't going to serve them personally. It won't last; it will fall over, or fly right back in your face in time. Create and foster an environment that serves and benefits the person you are talking to as well as yourself. Be clear in those thoughts, and they will serve you very well.

Know Who You're Talking to

To communicate with other people effectively, it's vital that you know the person or persons – the *audience*. This is where interpersonal skills come in handy. Everyone responds differently to different types of communication.

Knowing your audience has its benefits. It greatly guides you in developing your interpersonal skills. It always helps to prepare a little, to study something about your audience. Who are they, what do they do, what do they want, what moves them?

This allows you to tailor your message so that it really speaks to them. *The audience must benefit from the communication.*

Without receiving that benefit, the audience perceives the conversation as all about you, what you want. This won't go very far and most definitely doesn't last over time. It is here where you have the chance to develop great relationships that last. This can be staff, a client, prospect, family member or a complete stranger. In the end you are just so much more effective. If you remember just one thing, remember this: *When you communicate, never make it about you.* The harsh reality is that nobody really cares, and they simply won't hear you. It must be relevant *to them.* One way to accomplish this goal is to talk to people. Let's say you wish to talk to a prospect in business. If you understand what is important to them by researching what it is they do and how they operate, it will help you tailor your message to them. The ability to do this, to keep their best interest at heart along with an understanding of their business and the purpose they serve, is simply priceless.

Then talk to them, let them tell you about themselves. Ask them questions that engage them in telling their story. You have to be genuinely interested otherwise it just won't come across right. This skill can't be faked, not for long.

It isn't just business though, it is the same when trying to engage a group of friends in an activity, or a weekend trip with several families. It's in finding out what everyone likes, pulling the right people together with similar interests, similar place in life (with kids, without kids), perhaps calling them, taking the time to get to know them better. Learn what they like to eat, their habits, even their dislikes.

Preparing a little in these situations will go a long way. The event you wish to plan will have a better outcome, you will have more fun, your ability to create further events will escalate to new highs and it will have many other rewards that come with a successful outcome. Take the time to develop this skill and take it seriously.

The world is a place to serve. People wish to be served and those who serve well will reap benefits much beyond imagination.

Speaking the Right Language

You've probably seen advertisements for programs that promise to help you learn a foreign language. You may have taken advantage of one of these yourself and mastered another language. Being multilingual is a handy skill to have. In my opinion, though, the miscommunication between people who speak the same language is more of a problem than running into someone who doesn't speak your language. After all, what is the "right" language?

Especially between people who share the same actual "language" – English, Spanish, German or Chinese, for example – misunderstandings and the problems that arise from them happen frequently. A number of different reasons for this come to mind.

Vocabulary. Every group has its own set of words that it uses. Auto mechanics know all the parts of an engine, parts that may be unfamiliar to someone outside the industry. Young people have their own language that separates them from older people.

If you want to communicate clearly with another person it's important that you use the words they use, or at least words that they'll understand. Especially if you're a professional in an industry that has its own jargon, avoid using words that the listener may not know the meaning of. Sometimes people are too embarrassed to admit they don't know what you're saying, so a problem with miscommunication can become deeper and more serious.

Also, make sure that *you* understand the words you're using. The old saying applies here – *A little knowledge is a dangerous thing.* Misusing a technical term can not only embarrass you, it can create unnecessary obstacles to resolving an issue.

If you are not absolutely sure what a word or an acronym – a word made up of the first letters of a group of other words – means, then don't use it. It's wiser not to say something than to say it incorrectly.

Tone. Not just the words you use, but the way you say them, can have a profound effect on how the other person perceives what you say. We convey more information than just the words we use when we speak. Emotional content is also communicated, and our tone affects that more than anything else. Problems arise when we unintentionally use the wrong tone.

Tone can mean many different things – how loudly you speak, how fast you speak, whether you draw the words out or clip them off short, whether the pitch is high or low. This is not a scientific treatise on the study of voice or sound waves, so let's just say that "tone" is the method we use to convey emotion behind what we say.

Take into consideration as much of the environment as you can during a conversation. If the room is quiet, you might use a softer voice, speaking loudly might indicate that you're angry. On the other hand, speaking quietly in a loud room may indicate that you don't want the other person to hear what you're saying.

Some people speak loudly naturally, and they have to consider that when they have conversations. An important communication skill is being able to judge how the way you talk is affecting the other person. Try to find the appropriate volume level for the situation. (Remember this – if you *want* the other person to know you're angry, this technique works as well.)

The same is true of the rate at which you speak. Some cultures speak very quickly, and others speak very slowly. The listener's culture may determine how they perceive the conversation.

If you are naturally a fast talker someone from a slow-speaking culture may think you're excited, dishonest, or some other trait, whether it's accurate or not. The opposite is also true, a slow speaker may be perceived as dull witted or somehow mentally slow by a person who is from a fast-talking culture.

Think about how you communicate with others, and if you consistently use the tone that you intend. If you find yourself having misunderstandings with another person, analyze what tone you're using, and see if that might be the source of the misunderstanding. It's best to use a calm and pleasing tone, one that doesn't make someone want to run the other way, take a step back, or cover their ears. That, at least, is a good start. I'm sure you must have had conversations with someone that really didn't go that well – especially if you raised your voice or perhaps even started yelling.

Situation. Knowing the situation within which the communication is happening is the most important aspect of using the right language. Words or tone that might be appropriate in one situation can be completely wrong in another. It depends on the "emotional temperature" of the participants, the environment, and a multitude of other factors.

Good, clear communication takes all of these factors into consideration. When you are aware of the situation, with practice you can become better able to use the tools that you already have at your disposal.

The Other Perspective

Are you even interested in the other person's perspective really? Many people aren't. Although there can be many definitions, let's use this one for now – *Perspective is the point of view a person has, and what he wants from a conversation.*

I know this is extremely hard to look at, but I have found it to be true in pretty large numbers – people often care only about their own perspective. They will listen to someone else, but watch out if that goes against their own perspective.

Related to someone's perspective are their own personal likes, dislikes, desires and core values. If one person's perspective goes against someone else's core values, then that is going to hit a really bad note. This is another reason to choose your friends and associates carefully, otherwise you will find yourself continually confronted and challenged. This often turns to a sensitive reaction, critical and sometimes mean judgment of the other person. It stirs up fierce emotions in most people and can tear apart friendships, cause family members not to speak to each other and pretty much spills over every other area where there are people.

I have found there to be great value in going deep into myself on this one, and asking myself if I am really interested and open in hearing what another person has to say. Being open is really the pre-requisite to everything in this area. Being open to what the other person has to say, helps you not to judge them on their unique perspective on life.

I cannot stress enough the importance in the practice of keeping an open mind when listening to another person's perspective. The value to you is enormous and it is frequently overlooked. When someone feels you aren't listening to them or not taking their perspective seriously, or worse, judging them, you may as well not even have started. It will not end well and will leave everyone extremely frustrated. On the other hand, when you have mastered the ability to be non-judgmental when listening to others, the rewards are obvious. Here too people will in return want to listen to you and talk to you because they know they will be heard.

To remind myself of this sometimes harsh reality of perspective, I like to think of a book. A book has two sides, the front and the back.

When talking to someone holding a book in front of me, I see one side of the book. From my perspective I may be looking at the front of the book, reading the title. The other person sees the back of the book and does not see the title.

Our perspectives are much different but we are looking at the same book. What we each individually see is our version of the reality of that book. Although it is the same book we see things differently. We are both right, or both wrong, and in the end it really doesn't matter anyway, does it?

I always ask myself if arguing against another person's perspective is worth the agony it causes and if there is any reason for it. I also ask myself questions. Who am I doing this for? Is it self-serving (which it usually is), or does it really serve a purpose? Have some compassion on this, because it also goes for your own perspective. It is almost never perfect in another person's eyes. We all have to get along, if we wish to live productive and harmonious lives.

I am not saying you should never say anything, speak your piece, or just have a conversation. What I am saying is to be aware of what you wish to gain out of it. Learning better interpersonal skills involves thinking these things through, or at least becoming more aware as to why and when we would or should open our mouths. This is especially true if we wish to get another person's support for something we wish to achieve.

A place I learned to put in a strong version of my perspective was in my business, where I not only knew what I wanted to achieve, but also knew that I had the background and experience to hold tight to my perspective. If I didn't advocate for my dream, then who would? However, that strength wasn't effective on the days when I became louder or even mad when others didn't like my perspective, or had something to say against it.

Today I allow another person's perspective to be a part of the conversation, because there is value in considering someone's perspective, especially that of a team member, a partner or a client. At a very minimum I try hard to acknowledge their perspective and thank them for their input. What I have learned, though, is to maintain a balance, because I am the one who will ultimately be judged on my leadership to the result of the company I am currently leading.

It is important to learn this balance when interacting with others in situations where everyone has an opinion. Navigate through this carefully and respectfully. Doing this will provide value to all those around you, as everyone wants to be heard and validated – including ourselves.

Getting Your Point Across

Sometimes, we're not sure that the other person gets our point. You may ask yourself: "Are others even listening and understanding what it is I have to say? How would I know?"

There are several cues to watch for that will give you some indications if you are getting your message across in a way you wish to do. Following are four of them.

Look for verbal acknowledgment. The kind where someone gives you feedback and gives you an indication that they have heard you. Sometimes you will not get verbal feedback, so you may need to ask for it. Verbal acknowledgment and listening skills do not come easily for most people. If you want to know, ask for it.

If you don't like what you hear from the other person, then don't get mad, use it as valuable feedback indicating that you are not effectively communicating in a way that the person in front of you can or wants to hear.

This goes back to knowing who you are talking to, why, and if you are being precise, brief and interesting enough. Asking for feedback really can be eye-opening and should be looked at as a highly valuable skill. Don't reprimand people who give you feedback, especially if you ask for it. It is another component of becoming more aware of your own effectiveness and is the only way you can really improve your skills. Don't miss this great opportunity for growth.

Look at the end result. If things don't turn out the way you wanted, your project didn't make it on time, you had different dates on the calendar, a different understanding on the problem or some other issue, then you know you missed something.

If it gets to this point, then it is typically not the best time to learn that someone wasn't listening or that they misunderstood all or part of your message. It is much simpler if caught at the beginning through verbal communication, not to mention probably cheaper if money or time is involved.

Here too something to look at is having it get as far as a missed result or target. This is excellent feedback to effective communication, and it would serve greatly not to simply blame the other person, as this will not move you any closer to getting better at communicating. We so often just turn to someone else and blame them for the problem, but here too the harsh reality is to look inside.

Touch. Having someone reach out to you, touch your shoulder, back or arm is also a good indication that someone is paying attention to you. This shows engagement in the conversation. Some people don't like being touched, especially by strangers, but try not to react as you may be dealing with someone more kinesthetically inclined, someone more in touch with the feelings side.

Eye contact. If someone has eye contact with you and doesn't wander off in every direction then you can be pretty sure that they are engaged in the conversation. Here too though, you have to realize that not everyone can do this very well. Many people have problems looking into other people's eyes. Everything from nervousness to feeling insufficient, being scattered in too many thoughts or some other reason can prevent what you consider good eye contact.

All these examples offer some indication that you are being listened to. They all play a part in measuring your effectiveness, but they are dependent on many factors. The main thing is not to assume anything. The trick is to confirm, ask, and listen so that you know you are on the right track and get to a most effective communication path that is right for you, one that generates the right results and leaves everyone feeling good about themselves.

Are You Listening and Paying Attention?

Listening to someone seems easy enough on the surface. However, effective listening takes a much deeper understanding of what listening really is, and what it is not. Recognizing the importance and seeing the relationship in respect to how essential it is to getting what *you* want is of vital concern to you. Otherwise you might as well be talking to a wall and save yourself and others the agony and emotional drain.

The result of effective listening is that you will receive recognition and respect. It also shows that you really care for what someone has to say, that you value their views and experiences – in other words, their perspective.

Most people always care more about themselves being heard and listened to than in listening to another person. That's simply human nature, each of us seeking relevance in the world.

Walk into a networking event somewhere, or even a party, and see how many people actually ask you questions about yourself that go into any depth or which reflect genuine interest. You will find that if you ask someone a question they just go off into a whirlwind of conversation about themselves – often in so much detail that you start looking for a way to escape. Knowing this, and working with it, is very powerful as you can use it to your advantage. You can learn more about them, or about something they have learned.

Effective listening means paying close attention and not wandering off in thought, looking around or picking at your nails. If you find yourself doing anything like this you are not listening, no matter what you tell yourself. Multi-tasking is just not possible if you are truly listening.

More common – and so maybe even worse – is when you are thinking of your response while the other person is talking. How can you really be listening, if you start formulating your response and either start interrupting, or can't wait to respond with your "well thought out" response?

This behavior is a sure sign that you really don't care what the other person has to say. I know it's hard to look at yourself in this light, but it's true. It should tell you that you're putting more importance on yourself than on the other person. We have a personal choice to make – it's the answer to the question, "*do I like this about myself?*" In your heart you know if you need to change or not.

Other questions to ask yourself:

Are you getting what you want because of your position or title (boss, man of the house, parent)?

How is your relationship with the other person?

Do they want to be around you if they don't have to?

Do they do it?

Have you asked them if they feel listened to?

Answering these questions doesn't come easily, but doing so is valuable to moving forward in life and getting more of what you want. *It isn't always about you.* If this resonates with you, do yourself a favor and put some effort into improving this area.

Picking up physical cues is another skill well worth learning. Many of the same cues you may use when seeing if someone else is paying attention also apply to you. Becoming aware of your body language has many benefits.

You may want to become more aware of appearing to let your mind wander, possibly by actions such as looking around, picking on your fingers or some other nervous action. These are signs that you need to change something.

Either ask questions or refocus. One technique I use is to focus in on something of that person that sticks out to me, perhaps something I like about that person. Something around the face, maybe the eyes, is always a good place to start. This helps refocus your attention to the person, and helps you pay closer attention.

Learn the skill of active listening. Active listening is when the listener illustrates what the other person said. It is a great way to both clarify what you have heard as well as to acknowledge someone. This technique is worth its weight in gold and worth practicing.

Another technique is to ask clarifying questions. Try not to interrupt but ask them when it is fitting. This shows the other person that you are paying attention and that you care what they have to say. It is at that point you are more engaged. It's vital that you ask questions that are relevant to the subject being discussed.

Although the number of questions is as large as the subjects that can be discussed, one way to ask questions that clarify is to start your questions with *who, what, when, where, why* or *how*. Beginning questions with these words leads to more discussion of the topic and a greater exploration of related matters.

Paying attention to the other person's cues is equally as important, because you will be better able to gauge how they feel about your level of engagement in the conversation. Do they feel you are paying attention? Are they comfortable, frowning, wandering off? Perhaps even ready to jump at your neck? These are all good things to watch for. Recognizing conversational signs will allow you to make adjustments to your conversations and add tremendous value to your interpersonal skills.

Courses and seminars on improving your communication are offered all over the world and good training is always a worthwhile investment. It will go a long way in assisting you in getting more of what you want out of life, which usually comes out of successful dealings with other people. Effective communication is a key part of the equation.

I make it a point to seek out events from time to time that keep me moving forward and learning more on this subject, because you can never learn enough. In fact I have found that as soon as I think I have learned enough, then things start falling apart in some way or another. That's when the ego takes over, and I make it a point to try to keep my ego in check as much as possible.

One thing I like to remember is that we have two ears and one mouth. This reminds me to listen more and talk less, even though at times it's not easy. This just takes practice and a continuous desire to improve. This desire alone will keep you going, even when you mess up from time to time. It's another component of leadership, and just like anything else you want to master, when you keep getting back up again, failure is not a lasting effect.

The rewards are well worthwhile.

Failure represents bumps in the road. The size of the failure really doesn't matter. Here is a motto paraphrased by someone I know: You will experience failure on your journey to success, so "fail fast".

CHAPTER EIGHT

An Opportunity for Every Problem

There are constants that define our existence on the planet. Human beings share certain characteristics that make them human. One of those characteristics is that almost no one ever leads a trouble-free life. For everything we want, there are opposing forces of some kind. Random events occur which throw obstacles in our way.

If we accept that problems of one kind or another, of varying degrees of difficulty or impact on our lives, are a natural part of life then we are headed in the right direction to make our lives simpler; "simpler" in the sense that we don't waste energy bemoaning the fact that a problem has arisen. The philosophy of "problems arise as a part of life" puts you in the mindset that helps you resolve the issues more quickly, easily, and the problems that do arise have less of an impact on your life.

Problem solving is one of the most essential skills in life. Regardless of who you are or what you do, you will face obstacles. How you deal with such challenges will often be a determining factor in how successful you are in life.

While problems come in a wide variety of shapes and sizes, the following chapter will provide general guidelines and concepts to put you in the right direction.

If you are moving forward in life and achieving your goals, you are bound to hit some obstacles from time to time. They can come in the form of minor annoyances, or they can be like running into a brick wall. We have to accept the fact that nothing is ever perfect. I don't believe life is supposed to be that way anyway. If humans didn't have challenges, we would get bored and probably interfere with one another more than we already do.

What is a Problem?

A problem is basically just an obstacle. A problem can, and will, show up in pretty much every aspect of life. In business a problem can come in many forms – everything from getting started with a brand new venture, to trying to keep it alive, to getting out of a venture gone wrong.

People who get up every day and tackle their obstacles will encounter resistance in the world around them. The average person just doesn't want to face being uncomfortable and deal with problems, and they try to avoid them or pretend they're not there. People who try to avoid problems discover that their problems follow them. There is no real way to get around them. In fact, avoidance of problems quite often tends to make them even bigger. It's a weird phenomenon, but it's true.

In my twenty-plus years of self-employment, I've met a lot of people and some of them were people who I thought "had it easy." They were the ones I wanted to meet and learn from! As you might expect, once I got to know them better, I found that it was not any easier for them at all. Even multi-millionaires had problems that I wouldn't have wanted to trade my own for.

Once I accepted this fact and stopped looking around believing that everyone else's life was so much better than mine, it finally got me to a place where I could actually grow. Problems are just part of life and the more we can accept that and work with this fact the faster we can start working towards our goals in life and actually have a chance to achieve them.

In fact problems really are opportunities to make discoveries, to get out of your box, to do something different. During some of the world's worst economic times, many of the most powerful companies have emerged. Companies like Intel, Microsoft and Hewlett-Packard are just a few of them. I have found that during hard times people tend to get more creative and where creativity exists, innovation isn't far behind.

In our personal lives it isn't any easier. Problems come up constantly, with your spouse, partner, kids, or neighbors – and almost always at the wrong time. I really hate when problems come up on a day when I plan to go and have some fun. It can start with the kids fighting in the back of the car, then escalate to an argument with my spouse, and result in never making it to your destination, with a flurry of negative emotions by the time you get home. What was supposed to be restorative and relaxing has turned out to be anything but.

Problems are simply inconvenient all together. They stir up emotions, cost money and sometimes seem so overwhelming that all you want to do is roll over and go back to sleep. Problems also get in the way and are never convenient. They cause delays to the things you really want to do. They sometimes seem like a mountain that you are supposed to climb in one leap.

I think we all can agree that preventing a problem, or stopping it before it escalates, is well worth the effort. Even slowing down an emerging problem is a great help. Preventing a problem requires some planning and like anything else it takes some time. It takes thought and anticipation.

In business I try to anticipate all the things that could go wrong in order to build some redundancy around a potential risk or problem that could emerge. I also embrace the same philosophy in the products and services we offer to our clients. Spending time planning every move has proven itself worthwhile in many ways. That approach seems logical, but based on what I've seen, people don't spend enough time planning things out. I see it everywhere and it sometimes really scares me, especially when situations arise where it becomes obvious that a lack of planning lies at the root of an issue.

I like to consider the worst case scenario and then make sure I am familiar enough with that worst case to the point where I feel confident that I could handle it. Simply thinking it through seems to take the sting out of a problem that comes up. It doesn't catch me off guard (like a deer in the headlights) and I tend to move through a problem more conscientiously and more level headed.

Approaches to Problems

There are different ways to deal with problems, some more effective than others. Every situation is unique and with its own set of circumstances. What you will find, however, is that there is an appropriate approach that is most effective in the solving of a problem, you can:

Ignore it. You can ignore a problem. This alternative may come as a surprise. Ignoring problems really does seem to add fuel to your troubles. Have you ever tried ignoring your wife when she has something to tell you? Or ignoring your kids when they want something from you? How about ignoring a friend who feels you acted irresponsibly on your last outing with them? These are times when ignoring an issue is sure to get you in hot water.

However, there are occasional times when an issue arises and either the time or situation is such that handling it right away doesn't yield the best result. This could range from handling an emergency situation on a project at work due to an error of another staff member, to a problem at home with your neighbor.

This usually isn't the time to reprimand that person, as it will add fuel to the fire and make things even worse. In such situations, it's also a good idea to allow things to cool down and approach the problem with a clear head. Ignoring a problem and its timing is one option that you have to weigh out sometimes, and although ignoring problems usually doesn't give you desirable results, there are times when it is simply the best choice.

Delegate it. Sometimes the best person to solve a problem is – someone else. In some cases it's appropriate to delegate the problem to another person. It's not a bad idea but it doesn't work for every problem, especially if it's something you personally should be handling.

Sometimes you may be stuck on a problem and it takes a different pair of eyes and hands to solve it – one of those cases that just don't seem to be resolvable, may be avoided for a while. A situation such as that might best be delegated to someone who can seek the best possible outcome for you and the parties involved.

Delegating is a great way to leverage your time. Delegation is working with other people to achieve your goals. Sometimes that will mean asking someone else for help. Other times it will mean asking someone else to perform a task for you. If you choose to delegate a problem, there are some things to keep in mind. These ideas apply not only to those times, but any time you decide to delegate something to another person.

At this point, I want to give you a maxim that should never be ignored when delegating. *You can delegate authority, but not ultimate responsibility.* We're often tempted to do this when it's an unpleasant task that may end poorly. For you to be a true delegator, the consequences for the outcome should lie solely on your shoulders.

Different levels of delegation exist. The first level, and the worst (as far as delegation goes) is to do it yourself. This is called "not delegating." The main users of this level are those who don't trust other people to do the job properly. We all fall into this category at certain times, and on certain tasks. This level is appropriate in some circumstances. But it's important that you recognize that this level minimizes the amount you can get done.

The next level of delegating is to do the task yourself, but with someone's help. Besides giving you extra pairs of hands and eyes, this level offers the opportunity to train someone else in a particular area. And although the training aspect is very important, perhaps more important is the time spent with another person sharing wit and wisdom and letting the other person know that he or she is worth spending time with. Many rewarding father-son moments have come under the hood of a car. In business this is an act of leadership with many benefits. Teaching and working alongside another person will help them grow and allows them to get to know the job or function in a much more holistic way.

The third level of delegation is to help another person perform the task. This is the inverse of the previous level. At this level you are simply a guide aiding a person to reach a higher level of competency in a particular task or function. You may be able to use the opportunity to learn from another person. Great leaders are teaching and learning at all times.

The fourth level is to give someone else the task to perform independently. You ask the person to:

a) Perform a specific task exactly the way you tell him or her to do it.

b) Evaluate and decide what needs to be done, come up with a plan but don't take any action without presenting the resolution or game plan first.

c) Evaluate and decide what needs to be done, perform the task, and then present the outcome to you.

All of these levels are appropriate at different times, depending on the level of trust you have in the other person's competence (ability to do the job) and dependability (trustworthiness you can place on them to do the job.)

Delegating is a way for you to multiply your effectiveness, both in completing the tasks and jobs which you decide need to be done, and in building relationships with other people. Showing the faith you have in another person by letting him or her help you achieve your goals boosts the self esteem and confidence of those you choose.

Change plans. Sometimes seeing a problem can be a learning experience. The questions that arise may be so profound that the best course is to actually change your plans. I like the idea of taking the high road whenever possible. So I sometimes head off another way and focus my energy on a much better direction, one that moves me past this most challenging problem. Changing direction is sometimes the best thing you can do. Of course, this is another option that you would choose only after giving the matter your full attention and considering the consequences. This option is not "giving up" or otherwise avoiding responsibility. It is a thought-out option that keeps you from hitting your head against a wall - which of course is ineffective.

Solve the problem. Then, of course, there is always the option of solving the problem. This is best done as quickly as possible so that you can put it behind you. Good problem solvers are those who have solved many problems before. The more you do it, the better you get at it, and the more comfortable you are with the idea of solving future problems.

A good example of using a problem as a chance to grow was of an experience with a past employee. He had been a loyal employee for many years and knew many aspects of our business. One day he gave two weeks notice that he was quitting – via e-mail. This impersonal communication, and surprisingly quick exit, stung a bit but we knew he wasn't the greatest communicator in the world so we let it go. We wished him the best in his new job that he said he was taking.

In the month or so after his departure, several clients cancelled their service with us. It didn't take long to figure out that our past employee was now competing and taking clients away.

We considered several options, including taking legal action. After careful evaluation and weighing out everything, we decided to take the high road and focus our energy on something more productive. We took the opportunity in an ugly situation to grow as a company and move closer to our goals as a much more mature technology company.

Our company is more grounded than ever in a clear purpose and is on track to bigger and greater things. We have a strong and growing team of individuals where each and every person plays an integral role in the process. The moral of the story is that the energy of a *problem* was turned into an opportunity by dealing with it in a productive way. Now, evermore focused on a much bigger picture, our entire company and team have a sense of collaborative purpose - that of not only supporting companies with their IT infrastructure, but focusing on tying technological innovation back to the human element in the form of personalized training through video, as well as constantly aiming to create awareness as to how a specific piece of technology impacts not only the organization but its people.

This satisfies the needs of both management and workers, as far too often we see technologies put in place to solve a problem that is more of a human problem rather than a technical problem. We help tie all this together. We often refer to this as aligning technology to meet specific business objectives.

To think that this all started out with a "problem", and how a problem has helped us not only create enormous value to our customers, but as a company we now have a systemized vehicle that enables our staff to grow as individuals not found in the average company. What we learn and discover internally we then bring back out to our client in ways that support our customers far beyond technology.

The Nature of Problems

Before you can find a solution to a problem, it's important that you consider the nature of your situation. Many times more harm than help is done by leaping right into working on a problem. A little reflection, thought and contemplation can make a huge difference. A few thoughtful actions are worth more than a flurry of failed efforts.

In solving a problem, steps to take are to:

- Determine that a real problem actually exists
- Analyze the problem
- Decide the best solution

These steps are simple enough, but omitting any one of them can cause you to apply a less than effective attempt to solve your problem.

Determine that an actual problem exists. As I mentioned earlier, sometimes what we think is a problem is merely a distraction from other, more important things. How many times do we make a mountain out of a molehill? However, actual problems can have a profound effect on what you're trying to accomplish. It's important to differentiate between the two situations.

Often you can use *measurements* to see the severity of a problem. Some problems might move the needle of the "trouble gauge" just a fraction, while others make the needle swing wildly. If your sales don't reach expectations, if manufacturing or service times are too slow, if product is disappearing without explanation – you have a problem. What these examples have in common is that you wouldn't know about any of them if you didn't use measurements.

Another way to find if there is a problem is to use *milestones*. Milestones are markers or stages in a process that tell you how far you've progressed or how much further you have to go. When you are implementing a plan, you may have a schedule in your mind, or possibly even written down, that goes something like, "By Friday, we'll be at *this* point, then by next Wednesday at *that* point, and in two weeks we'll be finished."

You can also use the methodology used in project planning and setting goals - called "S.M.A.R.T." goals:

"S" – stands for *Specific* goal

"M" – stands for *Measurable* goal

"A" – stands for *Attainable* goal

"R" – stands for *Relevant* goal

"T" – stands for *Time-bound* goal

If you have not reached the expected point by the time expected, then the problem likely needs to be addressed. Again, the particular situation will determine if the problem is small or large, and your response should be appropriate.

In determining if a problem exists, you may also depend on *forecasts*. Forecasting is an art in itself, but for our purposes it merely means looking ahead and seeing where you expect to be. A simple example would be if you were in charge of planning the company picnic on a particular date. You check the weather forecasts and discover that it's supposed to rain. You have a problem.

Analyze the problem. Once you've determined that a problem exists and that you need to react, it's time to analyze the problem. This is best done by asking questions:

Where does the root cause lie?

What is the problem? Is it clear or are there things not lining up?

Why does this problem exist? How did it develop and what happened?

Who is involved? Has anyone taken responsibility?

When did this problem develop? Over time or suddenly?

Are there any ideas present to resolve the problem?

Who is best qualified to solve the problem?

By asking yourself these questions you can more orderly determine how to obtain the best solution to the problem. Look at possible options to resolve the issue at hand. Writing them out will provide a better overview, especially with more complex problems. The simple act of writing your options down on paper helps gain clarity of the issue. Soliciting the help of others and brainstorming can also help with a broader scope of ideas. It all helps you see the bigger picture.

The more detail you can put into the answers to these questions, the better. It's often easy to slack off and be satisfied with a short answer, but especially with more complex problems you find that each layer of answers uncovers other questions to ask.

It's important at this point not to fall into the "blame game" with a lot of finger pointing. That does nothing to move the process forward so that you can get on with business. Be willing to solve the problem in a productive way, a way that serves you long term.

See this as an opportunity to change something that obviously has not worked. Is there something to be learned? Try not to blame others, because this only avoids getting to the root of the problem. Before you try to implement any sort of solution you should thoroughly understand the problem.

Determining the Best Solution

The most important attribute you can have in solving a problem is to maintain a positive attitude throughout the process. Going at it with a negative and pessimistic outlook is almost guaranteed to produce a second-rate solution. Effective problem solving calls for a can-do attitude, an act of leadership. A good leader will navigate through all problems knowing that there is going to be a good outcome before he even tackles the problem itself. A great leader will do it swiftly and courageously leaving everyone involved feeling good about themselves.

It's at this point that it helps to have other people involved in finding a solution. You need both people with technical information or precise details and stakeholders who have a vested interest in the outcome. Both groups bring a perspective to the table which helps make the final solution better.

Factors exist which should be considered when trying to figure out a solution. A big decision has to be made on the *consequences* of various courses of action. Everything from "do nothing" to "take massive action" will have some sort of consequence. The judgment comes when you have to decide if the result is acceptable or not.

Sometimes there are various solutions that are good and you have to choose among the most sensible options at hand. Other times, the solution is the one that prevents the most damage. Regardless of the situation, the consequences for various actions have to be taken into account.

Another factor is the *price or cost* of a solution. Sometimes – maybe even usually – the perfect solution carries too high a price and a lesser solution has to be chosen. The price may be in terms of dollars, man hours, energy, risk or some other factor. The price may be that another problem has to be set aside to handle this one.

Whatever the price of the solution, always remember that *there will be a price*. What you have to decide is whether the solution is worth the price that you will have to pay.

Related to this point are the *resources* you will have available to devote to a solution. Suppose it is a project that's behind schedule – do you have the extra people to devote to it to bring it current? Your office copier is broken again – do you have the money to buy a new machine? If you fire that problem employee, do you have the personnel to take up the slack?

One resource that is often overlooked is the ingenuity or creativity of the people around you. Most people have skills or talents that are not well known to the rest of the world. Ask around and see if someone you know has the particular attribute you need to solve the problem. Especially with complex situations, making a change in one area affects other areas. Keep this in mind as you look for solutions – the *effect* on the rest of the organization. For example, if you use resources to solve a problem, that might create a problem in another area that was counting on those resources.

This is another reason to involve other people in finding a solution. They will naturally look at it through the filter of their own experiences, or even self interest. They may have legitimate objections to various solutions that you propose.

The Right Way to Solve a Problem

Once you have determined that there is a problem, and that it requires your attention, how do you decide what to do? Look at the effort and energy required to solve the problem in relationship to the options you came up with. Could a problem be solved simply by trying harder? This is often the first (and sometimes only) solution proposed by higher-ups, when the effort and energy comes from subordinates. Many problems can be solved by devoting more energy and work – but think about *who* will have to put forth the effort.

Is it possible to remove obstacles that are preventing progress? There is a system of problem-solving called *force field analysis*. This method is based on the idea that for every solution to a problem, there are opposing forces. For example, if you want to cut business expenses, you might consider discontinuing your office internet service. However, you use the internet to stay in contact with clients. The solution – cancel the internet – meets the resisting force of the internet's usefulness for staying close to clients. The answer is to try to remove the resisting force.

Could you cancel another expense and keep the internet? Can you find a less expensive internet service? Can you replace the internet with another method of communication? Finding a solution to the resisting force is important in that it makes implementation of the solution easier and more successful.

Sometimes the best solution involves a change of direction. If you are hiking in the wilderness, you may see on a map that the shortest route is a straight line. Following that line, you suddenly come upon a canyon that is hundreds of feet deep. Unless you planned to do some rock climbing, the best solution is a change of direction.

Many problems require you to make some sort of detour to reach your goal. Problems are feedback on the progress of your current plan. No plan is perfect, and even the best ones may require some alterations or adjustments to work.

When you analyze your problem, you will ask what resources you have to devote to the solution. The main resources that people can apply to a problem are *time, energy, money* and *brainpower*.

Time is a finite resource, and each of us has the same amount of time. The difference is in how we deal with that time. "Time management" is actually *self* management. What you need to decide is how much of your finite amount of time are you willing to expend on resolving the problem.

When solving a problem, energy is a combination of time, attention and effort. You may be able to devote an extraordinary amount of attention and effort to finding a solution for a brief period of time. You may be able to devote a little attention for a long time. A group of people may be able to apply themselves to a solution, thus providing more energy. In either case, you are expending energy to resolve the issue.

The easiest resource to measure is money. For good or bad, money is a major part of our culture, and often it can replace one of the other resources. Whether you have plenty of money, or not enough money, can determine what course of action you need to take.

Brainpower is knowledge, experience, creativity or anything else that a person brings to the table in finding a solution. We pay experts a lot of money to apply their expertise to our problems. We call the plumber, the IT technician, the house painter, and we deliver our vehicles to the mechanic at the garage. Expertise is a valuable commodity, and a resource that should not be ignored in finding solutions.

When it comes time to apply these resources, you don't want to squander what you have. Proper analysis of the problem can direct you to where and how to use your resources. This is often like a conductor directing an orchestra, with every component working in harmony with the rest. Remember, though, that the conductor works from a written score that has been meticulously thought out.

You may not need all the resources available to solve a problem. This is when you will determine which resources to apply and in what quantities. If you use the philosophy of "keep it simple" you will usually be on the right track. Again – don't waste resources.

You will also want to make sure that important things are taken care of first. Establishing priorities is absolutely vital to successfully solving problems. Is there a situation which has a profound effect on other parts of the organization, the project or the plan? Is there a scarcity of resources?

Many times we find that we don't have the resources in the right quantities to implement the perfect solution. It is at these times that allocating resources for the most important tasks is critical.

Opportunity Through Problems

I have the type of personality that makes me want to know exactly when and where a problem developed. I make every effort to use sometimes painful situations to learn the lessons I need to learn. Going through life with that kind of attitude has helped me tremendously in moving forward and past the toughest problems. It took some courage to get through some of them as I really had to take a good look in the mirror and take some serious responsibility.

I make every effort to be realistic. It's not productive to deny the truth of a situation. When you have made a mistake, it pays to own up to it and move past it. When looking at a problem I keep in mind that my perception is based on my own biases, prejudices and thoughts. I go to extra trouble to look at things as accurately as possible. There are no winners in the blame game.

Today I take problems head on and fast. All that being said I have learned extremely valuable lessons in this process. I am grateful to have had the courage to keep going when all seemed lost. I have, through this process, rekindled my love for my work and expanded my own capabilities. I'm able to do something different – but still stay close to what is important to me.

The funny thing is that it was in the same business. I had completely changed the concept of my business because of the lessons I had learned in what went wrong, the problems that evolved and challenged me so much. Looking in the mirror and taking responsibility for every problem no matter what, has changed the outcome of my life. I often find myself using the following formula when speaking to others that have a hard time looking at their problems and especially when it is time to look in the mirror.

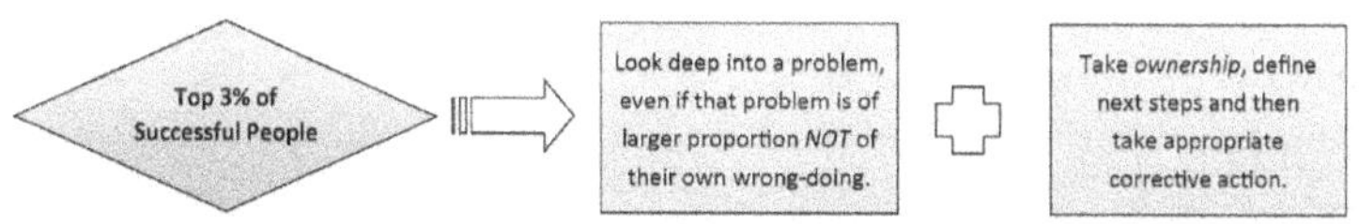

Only the top three percent of successful people are courageous enough to face, take ownership, and make efforts to improve on a problem that may only represent five percent of their own wrongdoing.

In other words, if you want to be in the top three percent of successful people in the world, you had better learn to look for that five percent where you could have done something different on a problem that was 95% someone else's fault. Just a subtle reminder - being right doesn't solve problems - taking action does.

Was it Truman who said "the buck stops here?"

Learn to see a problem as a gift and get ever better at tackling these problems in a constructive manner and the world will shape itself in a much more desirable form. Don't expect things to stay the same either. It's just not the way it works.

An example of growing because of a problem was learning how to handle the loss of a client. It often took all of my courage to ask the reason they chose to leave. I could have easily blamed our staff for messing up a project and blamed our customer for not being understanding or for being "difficult".

Instead I looked at what I, as the company's leader, could have done differently to head off these problems earlier. Could I better train my staff to better align expectations to our clients? Could I create better systems and the ability to measure developing problems? I took the opportunity to answer "Yes, we can improve." That answer has made our company better. I can honestly say that I would not have learned these valuable lessons without such experiences. They have helped to strengthen my character and bring more awareness around my own values as a leader – thus translating into the character and values of any company I am involved with today. As a whole we are simply more grounded and better aligned.

The Problem-Solving Culture

Since problems are a part of life, it helps if you can develop a culture of problem solving around yourself. Get around the right people. Seek out people you admire or people who have achieved something you value. Surround yourself with like minded individuals that support your journey in whatever it is you seek.

Be clear about what it is you want, otherwise the wrong people will be in your room. Having the wrong people in the room will only tear you down and suck the energy out of you.

Try to understand that it takes time to be clear about your own goals, values and objectives and to have patience and don't expect overnight results.

Seeking out professional mentors can be a worthwhile investment. Like anything else, take the time to check out their references, and what they have done in their life. Don't follow people that just talk, have all the answers, but have done nothing themselves.

Build your support system all around you. It is worth the investment to visit a seminar or two every year. It keeps you challenged, keeps your mind open for new things and new ideas.

Find local groups in your community that support your values and help pull you up when things get tough. Everyone needs support – going through life without that is a life alone. Learn to ask for support as well as give support.

Often there is a direct correlation to not being able to receive support from others and our unwillingness to give that same support. We learn and grow the most from the interaction and experiences of each other.

If you're afraid of competition in business, or afraid to share your wisdom and perhaps lose your job, try to remember that *amateurs compete and professionals collaborate*.

A person or organization working within these guidelines will stand out from the rest of the crowd.

If you're in business, find the right stakeholders to support your mission. Don't just blindly submit to tempting offers. Take the time to get to know people. Develop your soft skills – communication skills, conflict resolution and negotiation, personal effectiveness, creative problem solving, strategic thinking, team building, influencing skills, etc.

Fortunately, I have found circles of support, built a support system around me and through this have discovered my passion is in helping others through what I have learned. My wish is to help ambitious people navigate less painfully through their journey toward success than I did. I enjoy the idea of being able to help others who have a burning desire and dream to do something – whatever it is that is meaningful to them – and succeed at it. The thought of this is exciting to me and gives me energy and fulfillment at every turn. In fact this is one of my main inspirations for writing this book.

Our environment does shape us, it builds our character. This is all the more reason to bring some awareness into our surroundings and assure the right people are in the room with you.

CHAPTER NINE

Call to Action

Congratulations – you're a success! You've arrived! All your dreams have come true and your worries are over!

Wouldn't it be great if that's all there was to success? You work hard, stay focused, and one day you're "there," where you wanted to be and all is right with the world. The problem is, once you "arrive" you find that success – although very nice -- isn't everything you had imagined. What in the world could be wrong with success? Nothing – if you have the right point of view about it.

If you view success as a fixed point on the horizon, and that it never moves, then when you get to that point you may feel lost. Especially when you've worked so hard, made so many sacrifices – in other words, you have truly paid the price – there can be a bit of a letdown when you achieve what you've wanted.

The reason for this is that when you've developed the habit of working hard you get used to that feeling. The drive to move upward is what motivates you. When you think you have finally arrived "there," then there is no more motivation. The emotion that has kept you going all that time suddenly has no place to go.

The answer, of course, is to set new goals. You will need to find areas that interest you and items on the horizon that compel you to seek them out. Otherwise, you will find that what you thought you wanted is not what you want – at least not everything you want.

Another misperception of success is that it will solve all your problems. Although you may eliminate some problems, others seem to crop up to take their place. When you don't have much money, you believe that if you had *more* money, all your financial problems would vanish. You don't realize at the time that the *types* of problems may change, but problems themselves are still around. Everybody has problems. They don't go away.

The Next Level

Having said everything I've just said let me re-emphasize something that may have been lost – *Success is great.* All things being equal, having more money is better than having less money; having more freedom is better than having less freedom; being able to do more of the things you want to do is better than not being able to do them.

What is not so wonderful is arriving at a certain point in your life and thinking that you can stay at that level forever. Life simply won't permit it. The world and circumstances swirl and change around you and if you are not actively trying to move forward, then you will begin to regress.

Working within those realities is key to achieving and maintaining a high level of success. It is also essential to acknowledge and appreciate milestones as you achieve them. It is *gratitude* which manifests your achievements into your life and allows you to enjoy them.

You can't enjoy something you don't learn to appreciate in the right light. We often are so goal oriented that we forget to stop and smell the roses. Forgetting to stop, and have gratitude for your achievements, is where we lose the ability to properly balance our lives.

Enjoy your success and celebrate. Then begin planning *now* for the next level of a worthwhile accomplishment. I've found in myself as well as in others that no matter what level of success you reach, you will seek further. Your direction and emphasis on certain values may change but the desire to create, experience or achieve new heights is never ending.

I like to look at it as *living* and that it is just part of being human and staying engaged in life. People who work within this framework seem to do quite well. They are constantly re-aligning their next level of activity to their bigger goals. They take time to celebrate, give gratitude and have made it a habit to actively appreciate the *journey* itself.

When you see a person operating at this level and successfully engaged in life you will take notice of a special spark in their eye. I love it every time I meet one of those people. You can just feel that they are excited and engaged in life. They give me energy to keep moving forward in my own life and give me hope that others can also.

So always keep moving - it is time for you to renew the energy you displayed earlier, make preparations, align your actions with your bigger goal, and then *take action* again.

Why is immediate action important? First of all, because nothing ever happens without action. To shake off the stagnation that can happen when you have reached a particular goal, nothing beats action. Setting a higher goal, then taking steps to reach it, is the easiest way to move along the path to further success.

Another reason to take immediate action is because there's really nothing else to put before it. The first stage of creation is thought, creating the vision of what you want to do, be or have in the future. The second stage is actually *doing* something to move you closer to making that vision a reality.

Let's face it, there are many dreamers in the world, but far fewer doers – people who take action to create their vision and achieve their goals. The only thing that separates the two classes of people is action.

Waiting to take action, especially after you have formulated your plan for the next level of success, is dangerous. The world is constantly changing, and if you create a plan but wait to implement it, the plan may be obsolete before you even get started. There are few things in life more frustrating than having a really good idea, only to find that you waited too long and the moment of opportunity has passed. That is the real importance of doing something now.

The sooner you put an idea or plan into action, the fewer distractions that can crop up. Most of us have an endless parade of things in our lives clamoring for our attention. Some are more important than others. Set the right priorities and rid yourself of activities that are really not that important to you.

If you wait too long to get started on those higher priority activities and those that add real value to your life, then this endless pile of distractions start to burden you as you realize you are just not reaching those more important goals.

As with anything that you want to do, if your idea is to achieve something, then it has to become one of your top priorities. Other things that are important (but maybe less so) have to be chosen selectively, because every one of those things that you choose to do with your time takes away from your plan of achieving your biggest goals. Taking action on the right things immediately can minimize the number of those other commitments that can pull you off course.

Most people are prone to hesitate and procrastinate. These traits, although not helpful, dominate the day for most people. Those who choose to succeed in life, who mean to do more with their time, understand that hesitation and procrastination are the enemies of achievement. Action that is taken right away, right now, eliminates hesitation and procrastination.

The Balance

Knowing when to take a break should also be part of your plan. Without it you will risk burnout that could cause the failure of your original plan. I've seen too many successful people on the road to achieving greater heights that never really managed to take a break. The effects can range from marriages ending and kids ignored, to the point that built up anger gets them into trouble.

There are also general life balance problems that cause stress, weight gain and other issues. This goes back to the previously mentioned concept of "stopping to smell the roses." Procrastination, on the other hand, is what stops you from reaching *your next level*. Even the doers of the world can, at times, reach a point of procrastination or maintaining the status quo. Procrastination can come at different times in the *doers'* life:

- during tougher periods where things just aren't going according to plan
- as a result of losing focus during times of personal imbalance (not taking a break)

If you have followed the plan properly, then you should have created a vision and implemented your plan with the proper mindset. The journey along the path of finding success should have been filled with joy. While the trip was not always pleasant – there are ups and downs in every path, after all – you should be able to take satisfaction in the fact that you are engaged in a worthy endeavor.

When you reach your goal, it is really only the logical ending to that one particular part of your life's journey. You made a plan and worked hard to accomplish your goals, so finding yourself at the point where you are successful should bring momentary pleasure. That moment passes, as all moments do, and then it is something that you did in the past.

As for maintaining the status quo, I mentioned before the danger in that. Life changes around you, no matter how hard you might try to keep it in one spot. Trying to hold on to a particular moment in time is fine, but without consideration of the future it means that you're stuck in keeping something from the past. Often people tend to hold on to achievements made in their life to the point that extreme dissatisfaction or disappointment creeps in during times of change in their environment.

You can change with the times (by creating and achieving new goals) or you can sink with the past. You may think that you want to "rest," but the question I have for you is this – What are you resting *for*? A momentary respite to recharge your batteries might be great and then you can take action. Rest is only a moment between times of action. If you're resting, make it serve a purpose, the purpose of action in the right direction thereafter – and the next chapter of your life. Most people don't last doing nothing for longer periods of time. When there is no plan, even during periods of procrastination, people take action on things – just not always as productive.

The Penalty for Inaction

You can wait the whole day through, looking for the perfect moment to actually do something, but when you're honest with yourself, you know that there is no "perfect" moment. There is only now, and the things that can go wrong if you wait.

As I've mentioned before, conditions can deteriorate. What was the perfect course of action now becomes a sure way to lose. Some of the best ideas have come too late and the moment passed by. Don't let this happen to you. Most people's biggest regrets in life are their moments of inaction - not action.

The biggest danger is *inertia.* Inertia is the tendency of an object that is at rest to remain at rest. That goes for people as well. We become complacent, lazy, or otherwise more inclined to do nothing. Because at first glance this seems to be so much easier and less work, with less stress, it is very tempting to indulge your inertia.

The problem, of course, is that by doing nothing, taking the easy way out, you actually can create more problems for yourself. All the success that you have achieved can slip away from you without your attention. The only solution to this dilemma is that you have to move forward.

The question then, for the person who has achieved success, is what to do next. How do they plan for the next stage of accomplishment? One of the best ways that I have found is to seek a *mentor.*

The Mentor

The word *mentor* originally comes from Greek mythology. When Odysseus left for the Trojan War he left his trusted friend Mentor in charge of his son Telemachus, whom he had a paternal-type relationship with.

In modern terms, a mentor is a more experienced person who serves as a trusted counselor and advisor. You are looking for wise counsel when you consult with your mentor. You want someone with the expertise in the area you need and the availability to ask questions.

Having a mentor is the combination of the best elements of other ways of learning. Having the proper mentor in your corner will accelerate your success like nothing else.

When you seek out a mentor, you are looking for someone who has done what you want to do in a particular area. A mentor may have great expertise in one area and almost none in another area. It's important that your mentor have the knowledge you want in the area you need help.

For example, you may want to improve your relationship with your spouse or significant other. You wouldn't necessarily want to take relationship advice from the four-time divorced successful businessman. His expertise lies in another area! Instead, the person who is in a healthy, happy relationship might be more useful in that particular area. Leave the successful businessman for another topic, such as reaching your goals in a career or the starting of your own business.

Your mentor will also be someone who has done what you want to do – they have "walked the walk."

The ideal mentor is also a motivated teacher – not necessarily in the professional sense, with a teaching certificate, but someone who is interested in sharing their knowledge.

Most people with practical experience are happy to share what they've learned along the way, and welcome requests to mentor. They know that by sharing their knowledge they are leaving behind something that can outlast them. Often they even seek out opportunities to share as an *act of giving back* through understanding the value, significance and impact a mentor had in their own life.

There are many specific ways a mentor can help you succeed. Here are just a few examples.

A mentor can:

- Give you guidance or suggestions on how to handle specific situations.
- Help draw out your strengths.
- Help manage your weaknesses.
- Help you with goal setting.
- Help you develop your plans of action.
- Introduce you to the right people or businesses.
- Hold you accountable.

Finding the Right Mentor

How do you go about finding the right mentor? As with everything else in your quest for success, you have to be aware of exactly what you are going after, and start to define your goals. Awareness is a trait you want to develop and display at every step. In this case, awareness means observing your world and being able to see what's going on around you. You need to be prepared and well-informed to find the right mentor.

Many successful people I have met not only seek out different mentors in different areas of their life, but also seek out new mentors in the same areas to get different perspectives.

First of all, of course, you need to know in what area you want to be mentored. Is it in relationships, health, career, fitness or finances? When you know the particular area where you want help, then it narrows the field of people who you are looking at for help. At this point, you can seek out mentors through your friends, partners or relatives to get their opinions of someone who is adept in your area of interest. Getting a referral often helps narrow down your search more quickly.

Besides seeking potential mentors through others around you, you can also read newspapers, watch television and read trade journals to find those who are accomplished in a particular field. Get to know them, their personalities and see if there is a fit. When looking for a mentor, look to those close to you first. The ideal mentor may be a relative, a neighbor or someone in your town. Geographic nearness is a great advantage in a mentoring relationship. It provides immediacy of contact and enables you to have more frequent face-to-face conversations.

For many people, though, the ideal mentor is not someone close. Especially in business matters, the ideal mentor may be in another city or even another country. A hundred years ago, mentoring relationships were often conducted by correspondence. The advantage of that type of relationship in those days was that people of the early twentieth century were expert letter writers. Often their correspondence was thoughtful, well-organized and contained prose that was almost poetry. The only disadvantage was distance.

Luckily, communication has never been easier. Using the internet, e-mail, cell phones, video, text messaging or online chat can make meeting with your mentor easy and convenient for both of you. You are no longer restricted by distance.

There is something to be said for knowing what you want and being prepared to receive. Often that perfect mentor tends to show up in your life at the right time and out of nowhere. Some of my best mentors appeared when I found myself engaged in areas I was interested in and trying to master. It is my experience that far too many people sit and do nothing, waiting and hoping something will *just happen* out of nowhere. It doesn't happen that way.

In fact today I find myself attracted to help those who are engaged and actually working hard at something. It's frustrating to work with people who are waiting for a free handout, as they tend to need a constant push to do anything, and stop at every obstacle. Mentors are people too. Some of the best ones won't even be tempted to help you if you're not actively pursuing your goal and have an open mind. In fact, the most life-enhancing experiences have come from times when I knew exactly what I wanted to achieve, and why. It was *then* when the best mentors appeared.

Mentors are not miracle workers. They are people who enjoy helping others learn from their experiences in life. Mentors join you on your journey in life. They give guidance, become your mirrors, provoke thought – but they don't give all the answers. Often people become mentors to give back – many don't get paid. You will find them in every walk of life.

Once you have found the proper person to be your mentor, how do you go about establishing a mentoring relationship? First of all, respect the person who you approach. That person may have limits on time or desire to be a mentor. Don't go into your approach with the idea that you can force someone to be your mentor. As useful as their knowledge and experience might be, it dilutes their effectiveness to you if they feel pressured to do something they don't want to do.

On the other hand, if you can demonstrate how such a relationship might be beneficial to them, then do so. In the ideal mentoring relationship, both of you feel as though you have profited from the exchange. You have gained knowledge and information from the mentor, and he has gained satisfaction in helping you.

The Mentoring Relationship

Earlier I mentioned that in the mentoring relationship each of you benefits. This is the concept known as *reciprocity*. The mentoring relationship is a mutual exchange of value for value. You, of course, are benefitting by gaining knowledge from your mentor. What you must do is find what is of value to your mentor.

Sometimes it's as easy as showing commitment to your work and desire to move forward.

In some cases you too may have information or knowledge that can benefit your mentor. Even in his area of expertise you may have an outlook or viewpoint that is of importance. Older mentors may value the judgments of a younger person, simply to get that person's opinion.

A truly successful person never quits learning and hearing another person's viewpoint – especially if that viewpoint is much different from their own – is sometimes of great value.

The passion and desire you show may also be of value to the mentor. Sometimes a person has a lot of experience in an area, but no longer feels the same fire he did when he first started out. By associating with you, your mentor may feel the drive and passion that he had when he was younger, and that fire may be what he needs to reach even higher levels of success. This is yet another reason why you should communicate your desire to your mentor.

Remember that in the mentoring relationship you are part of the process. You have to remain involved and participate. If you approach it as though the mentor is a servant who is there to dish up knowledge without any commitment on your part, then you have the wrong mindset. Each of you is there to benefit the other in some way, and you abuse the relationship if you try to take advantage of it.

Historically, the best learning has always been achieved with the help of a mentor. A rounded education is best accomplished through first benefitting from the wisdom and experience of a mentor, and then serving as a mentor to someone else. Plato served as a mentor to Aristotle, who then served as a mentor to Alexander the Great. This is the cycle of education that civilization has developed.

Is there any field in which you're involved that hard work wouldn't make you better? Is there anything at which you want to be successful that practicing your skills wouldn't enhance your chances for success? In your area you can become greater than those around you by simply outworking and out preparing them.

When you learn about your mentor, copy what they do. They are successful for a reason. Often we are limited with what I call *our box*. To break out of that box, we need something compelling enough to reach for, to risk for. A mentor often sees you bigger than you see yourself. They help you see things you don't see and confront things you may not always want to look at.

It is this combination that helps you break out of your box and grow. This process will create new experiences and allow you to reach new heights. It will create new patterns, thoughts and habits. In time you'll have advanced into a *new you*. You will take everything you learned and make it your own.

A mentor's field may be completely different from yours, but if you read thoughtfully you should be able to adapt what they did and make it work for you.

In some cases, of course, adaptation won't be necessary at all. You simply take what they did and work their strategy. It makes sense not to try to reinvent the wheel on everything you do. Look at what has been successful before, and reproduce or improve that strategy. You'll be amazed at how often you also reproduce your own variant of successful results.

When you think of successful people, often famous people come to mind, such as Lance Armstrong, Donald Trump, Hillary Clinton or the Dalai Lama. Some were successful financially and some were successful in other significant ways. Remember that these people were themselves once inspired and mentored by someone else.

Lance Armstrong is known today for his heroic and successful battle with cancer, after which he went on to win seven Tour de France bicycle races. Were you aware that Armstrong was mentored by Eddy Merckx, himself a five-time winner of the Tour? Armstrong certainly would have been a champion regardless, but it's clear that Merckx's help was invaluable to Armstrong.

While you don't want to have to coerce or convince a person to be your mentor, it is important that you exhibit desire and passion for the subject. You can't approach this as simply another "assignment" you're required to do to be successful. No one wants to be around someone who lacks passion for the subject.

Think about it. Imagine you were an expert in a specific area – let's say movie director. Someone approaches you to be their mentor. When you talk to them you find that they don't really know anything about making movies, haven't taken the time to go to film school, read books, or even own a video camera. They are only there talking to you because one day they woke up and thought making movies might be fun, or perhaps thought it would be a great way to make a lot of money. How would you feel about that person and would you have any interest in mentoring this person?

By being prepared, engaged and communicating your passion, you show respect for the mentor, their time and for their knowledge. If the subject is important enough for you to seek out a mentor, then you had better be prepared. Remember when the student is ready the teacher will often appear.

One of the major by-products of true success is that you become wiser along the way. You realize that no matter how much you may have learned, there is still much more you have to learn. The more successful you are, the more you know you have to learn. If you think you know it all, then you simply don't know enough.

This means that the truly successful person commits himself to being a lifetime learner. The education may be deep – learning more about a subject with which he's already familiar. It may be wide – learning more about a subject about which he knows nothing. Nonetheless, that learning will always take place when a successful person recognizes his place in the world.

Why does this learning have to happen? Because when you have worked hard to be successful and you've stayed true to your values, then you know that there is something better awaiting you and you want to plan for it. The only way to be prepared is to learn new knowledge, acquire new skills and figure out a way to put them to use.

In an earlier chapter I mentioned the importance of finding ways to further your education in different areas. In addition to mentors, look for books, tapes, seminars, and other methods by which you can become better equipped to do what needs to be done to reach further success. At this point, you are looking for inspiration and motivation as well as knowledge. Keep that in mind as you check different avenues of learning.

It's possible that when you work through the ideas and techniques in this book, you'll reach levels of success that you've previously only dreamed of. At times that success comes after hard work, slogging away at your goals and then suddenly – poof! – you've accomplished more than you might have thought possible.

It's at such times that we as human beings are susceptible to the trap known as "I've made it." We seem to forget everything that we've learned and every habit that we developed to get to the point of success. We basically sit on our laurels.

It might help if you understand that climbing the mountain and reaching the peak is not the end of your experience. You want to celebrate such moments, of course, because rewarding yourself for doing well motivates you to go on doing well. There is always reason to celebrate an accomplishment, be it small or large, and you should always take the opportunity.

The celebrating will eventually end, though, and you are faced with one of the biggest questions anyone can face – *what's next?*

A Revelation

You are not your job. For many people, this is a difficult concept to grasp.

With as many hours as most of us work, it's sometimes hard to separate our identities from our work. Whether you're self-employed or work for someone else, you put much of yourself into your labors and the line between work time and home time often gets blurred.

Regardless of what else it is, your job is primarily one thing – *it's what you do for money.* If you deliver letters you're a mail carrier. If you shoe horses you're a blacksmith. We're so used to identifying ourselves as what we do for work that we forget that the main reason we work is for a paycheck.

That's not all your job is, of course. However, the reason that I want to separate what you do from who you are is because, for most of us, our job is one of the least thought-out life decisions we make.

Some people plan out their career path carefully, of course, and work the plan all the way throughout their lives. For the rest of us, finding a job is hurried, panic-driven and our choice is governed by lower-level factors.

Personally, I think of a job as a place to express my creativity in something I enjoy doing. This changes over time and is as much part of life as everything else.

Over time everything you do will become routine. If it is to remain interesting, somehow you have to change it up a little.

I believe human beings need to grow and experience something new in order to maintain a good balance and interest in life. Thus, a job can be a great creative outlet and if combined with a purpose you are passionate about, could bring a great sense of fulfillment into your life.

Even if you are in the job that you were meant to have, fulfilling your life's plan, you can't define your entire life based on your job. Your job is simply one role that you play in your life. Other roles – father, mother, brother, sister, son, daughter – are as much, if not more, important than what you do for employment. Human beings are many-faceted. Even when the job is very important to them, it's simply one aspect of their life.

If you're not your job, and you don't define yourself by your job (or let the job define you) then the question you may well ask is "What is my job?" The answer for any job – whether you work for yourself or for someone else – is to provide value. If you're self-employed, then you already know the importance of providing value to your customers. By doing that you are on your way to the type of success you've planned for yourself.

If you work for someone else, you have to provide value to your co-workers, your managers, the company itself and, ultimately, to the customers. Whatever your task, your goal must be to do more than "just enough." By being the type of person who aims for excellence instead of average, you define the job, rather than let it define you.

All this having been said, in the back of your mind must always be the primary question: *What's the purpose of my job?*

First of all, your job provides money. It's what you do to facilitate personal fulfillment in many aspects of your life. The money provides for your family and other important things in your life. There will be times when you need to create an imbalance in your life. For example if you have a new baby, that baby will require considerable attention and care. Other parts of your life will be secondary.

In the same way, there will be times when your job is your "baby." If you are starting your own business, then the startup will absolutely require more of your attention and effort. Other parts of your life may have to receive less attention than it deserves. To a truly successful person in life that imbalance will be temporary. Although an occasional imbalance is necessary for the entrepreneur who wants to succeed in business or an employee who has extra duties thrust upon him, if your job consumes all your attention and time for an extended period you need to recognize the imbalance and make adjustments.

What's difficult for high performers to realize is that *job* fulfillment is separate and different from *self* fulfillment. A job should be rewarding and enjoyable. You should get a sense of accomplishment out of it. Ultimately, though, it is simply a part of your life that, as a whole, should be fulfilling. In other words, your work should be part of a fulfilling *life*. A fulfilling life is one in which you understand, pursue and achieve your vision, dreams, and desires, and perhaps even find your life's purpose.

The way you act at work will affect every other area of your life. Our true nature has a way of saturating every part of our lives, no matter how we may try to compartmentalize it. If you are a high achiever at work and devote yourself to doing the very best job you can, that attitude will come through when you're helping your child with his homework, performing maintenance around the house or trying to organize a bowling league. Make it a habit to give your all at work and you will soon find the rewards showing up in all aspects of your life.

You just have to become aware enough to apply *your all* to all other areas of life. It took me some practice to start seeing this connection and to slowly integrate all aspects of *who I am* and *desire to become* in all areas of my life.

Separating or compartmentalizing your professional life from your personal life takes effort. It takes energy – energy that brings you further out of alignment with your true self.

Have you ever had a friend whom you almost didn't recognize the first time you saw them in their work role?

Perhaps you even felt they were not their authentic self while in that role?

Life becomes easier when everything you do is part of a natural flow of who *you are* and when there is no difference in how you act in both a professional and personal environment. Simply – being you. That's freedom!

Performing your duties on your job is also part of the greater whole of your success journey. By now you understand that nothing in the universe is free. The job you do is part of the price you pay for your success. Giving your all in your job and career has a price to pay – going half-speed or giving it less than your best effort also pays a price. As we have discovered, the price for all levels of success *will* be paid. It's simply a matter of paying what you choose to pay or letting the universe decide for you.

The question of your job and your career is important because of one factor – you deserve to live the way you want to live. Whether you want financial security, a lavish lifestyle or a simpler life, your choice of career will affect your ability to meet that desire.

There are sometimes questions about whether someone "deserves" what they have or not. People who always take the easy way out, make the easy choice and avoid exerting any sort of effort will pay a price for their choices. It may be in the form of chronic anxiety over finances or an inability to keep a job, among other things.

For those who make the difficult choices, putting higher priorities over lesser ones, they are also paying the price for the choices they have made, which may very well result in a more comfortable or desirable lifestyle.

The Law of Reciprocation determines what we will enjoy in life. “What goes around comes around,” and never more so than in our work lives. There may be temporary discouraging moments, but they are part of the process of achieving success in life. In the long run, giving your all at work will come back to reward you many times over.

What kind of life do you want to lead? That question seems easy to answer at first, but deeper thought on the matter may well reveal many details that may even come as a surprise. In a sense we all lead dual lives. One is the life we are living, moment by moment, in the “now.” That’s the part of us that is aware, using our senses to get input from the world. We are always urged to “stop and smell the roses” along the way. Only you can get into a habit of stopping and relaxing once in a while to catch your breath, and perhaps most important - recognizing all that is good around you and being grateful for whatever you find - no matter how small.

The other “you” is the future you. While we must live life moment by moment, we also prepare for the life we will lead tomorrow, the next day, next year. It’s the perfect image of this future you that keeps you focused on the success that you will enjoy. This perfect image is the graphic representation of the lifestyle that you choose. Your job and career choices are resources to help you realize that perfect image.

What kind of lifestyle do you choose for yourself? How do you choose to live? The answer to this must be based on the goals and priorities that you have set for yourself. For your life to be fulfilling, you must act in alignment with those goals and priorities.

How do you choose to "live" at work? For it to be such a major part of your life, you have to be able to conduct yourself in a way that corresponds with your values and priorities. You should be able to abide by your principles. As you conduct your business, take into consideration the values that you have chosen to live by. Are you acting the same way in your career that you want to act in the rest of your life?

If you are having trouble reconciling your job with your principles, take some time to see what might need to be changed so that the two are in alignment.

Whether you work for yourself or for someone else, learn the habit of giving and receiving respect. In the urgency and deadlines of business, we sometimes forget to treat others the way we want to be treated. Respecting others indicates that you acknowledge their worth and that your own sense of self worth demands that same respect from others.

Learn to always strive for excellence, regardless of the task or job that you're asked to perform. Live for your larger goals. Few jobs are ever done perfectly every time, but if your aim is to be excellent, then no one can ask any more of you. Maintain that standard all the time and your reputation will be assured. Even if the task is simple, maybe even something that you consider "beneath" you, give it your all so that you will be ready to excel at those assignments that are more rewarding.

Love and respect the people you work with. The challenge is that all of them may not be lovable! Even if individuals act in a way that makes it difficult, choose to respect and value the humanity that abides in all of us. When you show your respect for other human beings, their reactions are not important – the quality of your interactions will improve anyway. You will have let them know that they have value.

Do your best to keep your work life and your personal life in balance. Separate your personal and professional life issues from each other to the best of your ability. Obviously there will be times when that is not always possible, such as times of advancement, job challenges, or tough economical times.

Remember that what you deal with inside - your issues and emotions - will spill out in other areas of your life. These cannot be successfully separated. Your job can be stressful and it can harm your personal life if you bring that stress home with you. Likewise, don't bring personal problems into your workplace. It won't help the personal issue and it can only negatively affect your work.

Balance – it's the key to enjoying the success that you've had and the success yet to come.

CHAPTER TEN

Staying on Course

There's a famous story about a vice president at IBM. The VP took the lead in developing a new product, a risky venture that wound up being an enormous failure, costing the company ten million dollars. IBM founder and CEO Thomas Watson called the man into his office.

Before Watson could say a word, the VP said, "I guess you want my resignation."

"You must be kidding," said Watson. "We just spent ten million dollars educating you."

Business guru Peter Drucker has said, "The better a man is, the more mistakes he will make, for the more new things he will try. I would never promote into a top-level job a man who never made mistakes. Otherwise, he's sure to be mediocre."

Although any given mistake may be avoidable, what is inevitable is that – you will make mistakes. The odds are good that at some time in your life, with constantly-changing conditions and information, you will formulate a plan that *should* have worked, but didn't.

Especially if you are used to being consistently successful, experiencing a setback can cause you pain. What truly successful people do, however, is find a way to recover and even prosper from occasions when their plans go off the rails.

It's one of the laws of the universe that nothing is ever as smooth as you think it should be. The ocean has waves, roads are bumpy, and human progress often slows to a standstill. Looking for a smooth road to take any action is looking for something that you may never find. Even with the best efforts however, if you look close enough you can see that the surface of a supposedly smooth road is still pitted and rough. It's all based on your perception.

I've said it before - personally, I would regret inaction far more than having taken action, simply because, without action, I would never know what could have been.

With that in mind, how should we view setbacks? It would be great if we could describe them as "backward progress" and feel better about it. Ultimately, though, we have to face the fact that we are further away from our goal than we were. At a time like that, how do you prevent yourself from falling into despair?

First of all, try to think of a setback as feedback. If you keep in mind that all you are getting is information, not a judgment, then it's easier to keep a setback in proper perspective. Thomas Edison, the inventor of the electric light bulb, worked for years to perfect a working model. The problem he had was finding the proper filament that would last long enough to provide a viable commercial product. Edison reportedly tried ten thousand different unsuccessful elements before he settled on the one that had the proper characteristics. When asked about these failures, Edison replied, "I did not fail. I found ten thousand ways that didn't work."

Use errors as feedback to correct your course. It's been said that a torpedo is sent toward its target in a straight line. By the nature of the sea, the currents and shifting conditions, the torpedo must be adjusted periodically to keep it on course. It may go too far one way, and then too far another. Eventually, however, with the adjustments, the torpedo reaches its target.

Your setbacks and mistakes are simply messages from the universe that you need to make adjustments. Sometimes the message is harsh, and hard to accept. Regardless of how it feels at the time, however, you can either ignore the feedback or you can pay attention to it and adjust your course.

Besides the message that you need to make an adjustment, setbacks can often offer you clues on what you need to do to improve. Weak spots in your process, your product or your approach to a matter can be more precisely pinpointed when you have the benefit of suffering a setback from it. That's one thing about suffering a setback – you can completely trust the information. Nothing is as convincing as the pain of a mistake you have made.

When you make a mistake of some kind, recognize your weakness as a human being and exercise your right to forgive yourself. That's often much harder than it sounds, and many people find themselves incapable of doing it at all. Unless you consider yourself something better than human, however, fallibility is built into your wiring.

If you have worthy values, based on always seeking positive solutions, then forgiveness should be part of your outlook. If someone else transgresses against you, make the choice to forgive them.

As Gandhi once said, "An eye for an eye leaves the whole world blind." Seeking out retribution against those who have committed an error is ineffective. Why don't you apply that same spirit to yourself? If you make a mistake that impedes your progress, you are merely showing the signs of humanity. Forgiving yourself is a higher expression of that same humanity.

If you forgive yourself, then you can forego the pleasure of beating yourself up unnecessarily. Seriously, expressing self criticism and punishing yourself is a waste of energy and of effort that could be put to more productive pursuits. If you amplify your errors in conversations with other people, you are doing nothing but hurting yourself further.

That's the one problem with beating yourself up over making an error. It tends to amplify the error. What was once a simple issue can become something more complicated and damaging simply because you are making it so. You are simply making a bad situation worse.

Even something like regret can drain your energy. Any time an emotion takes your mind off of reaching your goal, it is no longer useful. Regret is almost never useful. It's like an infection that can fester inside you, preventing you from doing anything productive.

The problem with regret is that it does not lose strength as you indulge it. Regret seems to feed on itself, until your error takes on mythic proportions in your mind. Regret is a focus on the past and blindness to the possibilities in the future.

The most important aspect of self forgiveness is to realize that any mistakes you made were made by a past "you." The person in the past didn't have the benefit of the knowledge you gained from your mistake. Learning from your mistakes is vital if you are to make progress toward your success. You can go back and analyze the times you have made mistakes, even in the distant past, and forgive that version of you.

If you do this little exercise, don't fall into the trap of feeling regret. On the contrary, forgive yourself and move on. Be grateful for the knowledge you gained from that mistake and resolve not to repeat the mistake again.

Perfectionism

One mistake that anyone can make is the trap of *perfectionism*. We talked earlier in the book about the problem of paralysis by analysis and how it can prevent you from taking action. On the other end of the process is perfectionism, or expecting unrealistically perfect results from your actions. Perfection is exceedingly rare, and the person who expects perfection is destined to be disappointed.

Although a good sounding ideal, perfectionism isn't what drives success. It is action and moving towards something. Perfectionism on the other hand holds you back, often resulting in incomplete projects. For example, take this book. It took me several years to get this done, often playing in my head. I finally realized that if it was going to get written I had to let go of the idea of perfection.

It is my experience that perfection – or as I like to call it ***mastery*** – is something you achieve over time by doing, learning and revising. Some of the world's greatest products evolve over a period of time.

Let me make clear that there is a difference between having high expectations and perfectionism. You should always strive for excellence in whatever you do. However, being dissatisfied with anything less than perfection will inevitably lead to feelings of discouragement and lower self worth. It also acts as a brake. I see far too many people unable to even set things in motion, and even fewer reaching their goals.

One version of this type of perfectionism is having a very specific idea of what will make you “happy,” or give you a result. The more specific your idea, the less possible it is for you to actually *be* happy or satisfied. Your unspoken message is *“Only this very precise combination of conditions will make me happy. If even one element is different, I can’t be happy.”*

Such an approach is especially damaging in relationships with people. If you are expecting perfect conditions in your relationships, then you are sabotaging your efforts before you even start.

Relationships involve other people and if there is one message that I have tried to make clear in this chapter, it’s that human beings are imperfect. Trying to fit an inflexible template over your relationships will destroy them for sure.

When you indulge your perfectionism, you are pushing out the good for the perfect. In other words, you may have a result that is completely acceptable on all levels, yet reject it because it doesn’t fit your narrowly defined idea of perfect. You therefore reject a perfectly good result because it doesn’t fit your template. Such a move is impractical, wasteful and dispiriting to those around you.

The worst part of being a perfectionist is that you can never be a winner. Even with a successful result you won’t be able to resist the urge to pick at it until you are no longer happy. “Yes, but….” you’ll say, until any pleasure you should derive from winning has been completely drained away.

Making Corrections

If you are in the position of having made a mistake, how do you go about correcting it and getting back on track? The first step is to recognize that you have made a mistake. Sometimes that's the most difficult part of the process. Once again, awareness plays an important role in your quest for success.

Having measurements to gauge how you are doing is useful when you want to know about a mistake quickly. Feedback from customers and partners can help. When you make an error, try to have a system in place so that you know about it as soon as possible.

If you are the type of person who enjoys numbers, then use them to see if you are moving forward or if you've stalled. Numbers don't lie – if your measurements don't match your projections, find out what's wrong and correct it.

Many setbacks can be avoided if you remain aware of where you are and what you're trying to achieve. That awareness is what makes wealthy people check on their investments periodically to see how they're doing. It's what makes pilots run through their checklist before every flight. Awareness is one of the best attributes you can ever have.

As mentioned before, establishing milestones can help you prevent setbacks. Stay on top of your numbers and you will find that things go much more smoothly. Use measurements – weight, time, dollars, number of sales – to provide you with markers along the way and you will instantly recognize if you are on schedule with your success plan.

Once you realize that you've gotten off track, how do you recover from a setback? First of all you have to become a problem solver. Think through the issue to determine exactly when and where you went wrong. Did something occur about the same time you lost your sense of excitement? Did a bad month throw you behind and you've never recovered?

Once you've found the cause, figure out what you need to do to get back on your plan. Decide if you need to make a major change or if you can tinker with your process to make sure it's working like you want it to. The most important thing is that you have the mind set that whatever it is, you're going to fix it. It is then when you are essentially unstoppable.

You may discover that you are working the wrong plan. You shouldn't have this problem if you have been honest in your answers and faithful to the plan, but occasionally you will have priorities that changed and now you need to alter your plan.

Something this fundamental requires an extensive reworking of your plan to encompass your priorities. Incorporate as much as you can of what you have done into the new plan so that you can start ahead of the game. Remember that the process is the same, regardless of what your goals are. Only the details change.

The most important thing about recovering from a mistake is that you don't compound it. Learn from your mistake and move on. You need to keep your focus on your ultimate goal, and endlessly playing over what you "should" have done, or "could" have done, will only make the matter worse. This often cripples people and sometimes causes them to become too cautious in making mistakes.

The Math

I like taking action and making mistakes, and view it this way – for every seven mistakes I make, I get three things right. An overly cautious person may only make two mistakes. Even with the same percentage he will have less than one thing done right. My result is three times greater.

This has been my personal experience. It's not that I take unnecessary risks. Through practice, as my experience in failures grows, I get better at evaluating risk. I have lots of data to pull from. Sometimes these lessons are costly, but it always balances out. My losses may be greater but so are my gains. In many ways, it's like playing the same game that started with a dollar bill, then a hundred, then a thousand and so on. The numbers get bigger, but the concept and mind set is the same.

Human Roadblocks

Often one of the first signs of success is when you start receiving criticism from those around you. Perhaps they are those who have given up on reaching higher goals in life. As you move forward, they often see themselves being left further and further behind, and sometimes you're just a painful reminder of the effects of inaction on their part. They often tend to do everything they can to pull you back. Don't let this happen. You've determined that you are going to be successful, and no one is going to stop you.

You'll hear variations on all the old programming that you've eliminated from your life. People who try to hold you back will push every button they can think of to stop you from reaching your goal. You'll recognize these people – they're bitter because they have given up on themselves. They'll try to hurt you with their remarks, as it often hurts them to see someone become more successful and prosper. The best you can do is to be mindful of where they are.

Support and Encouragement

You'll never go wrong when you follow your heart. You cannot only say you tried but know that you have, and through that have lived. Without that you can't even get close to reaching your fullest potential.

The people you want to keep close are those who encourage you to continue your ascent. These are the people who understand what you're trying to accomplish, and they will help and support you along the way. Positive people produce positive results, so surround yourself with those people.

The Balance in Relationships

Sometimes, however, even if it's based solely on the other person's perceptions, a relationship can be challenged, perhaps even damaged because of your pursuit of success. Neglecting a relationship is one of the most common mistakes successful people make.

It's easy to get caught up in your passion in reaching for the stars. That's why striking a balance, as discussed in previous chapters, is so important. Again, it's even good for you because reaching your goals and while disconnecting from the world will ultimately not give you what you are looking for.

Far too many, including myself, have learned this the hard way.

If you find yourself in such a situation remember that building and maintaining strong, fulfilling relationships with other people is one of the highest priorities you can have. When you recognize this has happened, it's time to do something that may be hard for you.

Apologize, sympathize and re-engage in other important areas in life.

What are you apologizing for? For neglecting to properly maintain an important relationship. If the other person feels neglected or discarded, then you've made a mistake, and your relationship has suffered a setback. A truly successful person recognizes the damage and takes actions to repair it. The first step in repair is to apologize and show that you care.

Remember that while a sincere apology can improve your reputation and relationship, an insincere apology can make matters worse. It's important that your apology results in the other person feeling valued. This can be shown in many different ways – mainly by taking some form of measurable action.

Assuming that you truly care about the other person the emotion behind an apology must be genuine. A good apology involves three steps. You must acknowledge the fault or offense, you have to express regret for it, and you must reinforce the worth of the person to you.

Done right, an apology can be both brief and effective. For example, someone who may have offended another person by devoting less time and attention than the relationship required might say something like this, "I realize that I have not spent as much time with you, or paid as much attention to you lately. I am really sorry for that, because our relationship is very important to me, and I wouldn't intentionally do anything to hurt you."

Remember the value of a good apology. After all, success without the ability to share with your loved ones is a very lonely and empty version of success.

History Remembers Success

As I mentioned before, it is human nature to make mistakes. That's not very comforting when you are in the middle of your problem – part of the nature of a problem is that it tends to distract you from the big picture. It's hard to think clearly and take a step back when you are emotionally engaged. However, even the greatest successes in the world have made terrible mistakes. History remembers primarily the successes over the failures of an individual.

Think about writers. Ernest Hemingway is considered to be one of the greatest American authors of the twentieth century.

His works are used as examples in writing classes and college courses. What he's remembered for, however, is a handful of novels and short stories. These few works represent only a small part of the huge quantity of stories and articles he wrote. What he's remembered for are the pinnacles of his success. Without taking away from his talent or reputation, let me suggest that Hemingway wrote hundreds of thousands of prose that were less than great. In fact, I'm sure that somewhere he wrote things that were downright awful.

Is Hemingway remembered for his awful prose? Of course not. People know him for *The Old Man and the Sea* or *For Whom the Bell Tolls*. His style is immediately recognizable by students of literature. His mistakes and terrible efforts are forgotten and ignored.

In the same way, you will be judged by your successes, not your failures. Consider Sanders, the founder of the Kentucky Fried Chicken restaurant chain. He worked at several jobs as an adult, eventually opening a gas station where he served meals. Sanders developed a recipe and method of cooking chicken that became popular among locals. He was given the title of "Kentucky Colonel" by the governor of Kentucky and began to present himself as "Colonel Sanders."

However, Sanders's restaurant/gas station depended on traffic for its business. When the interstate opened, his traffic dropped to almost nothing, destroying his business. Colonel Sanders had the idea of selling his chicken recipe to other restaurants. He used his Social Security check to finance his trips, and eventually established a chain of restaurants that we recognize today as KFC.

Colonel Sanders is not the first name that comes to mind when you think of failures. However, it wasn't until age of 65 that he found lasting success, and then only by virtue of previous setbacks. So you can see, human nature almost predestines that you are going to backslide and have setbacks. The most successful people in history have had setbacks, but you don't always know it from the history books. The lessons are taught on their successes.

Deciding that you are ready to get back on track is the biggest decision in recovery. What do you do next? What's the procedure for correcting your course?

First of all, you need to know *where* you are. This is when you make the decision as to whether you're where you want to be or not. If you have applied measurements, then it should be a simple matter. Are your numbers where they ought to be? Are projects on time and on budget? Is there a persistent problem that has not been corrected? These are all questions that will help you figure out where you are.

Next you have to analyze *why* you are where you are. Sometimes this involves the process of going back over your plan and finding the spot where things changed. Other times it means looking at persistent problems to see what caused them. This is a situation where your problem-solving abilities can really pay off.

Finally, you have to make proper plans to correct what went wrong. This can be one of the harder steps, because you are invested in the original plan you designed. Moving beyond where you are and to the next level of success requires that you have the strength to take action in the proper way. Remember, your success came to you in large part because you were willing to do the things that other people couldn't or wouldn't do.

The Danger of Blame

A very human trait, but one that inevitably does damage, is trying to place blame. The blame game is one in which there are no winners.

When you find that you have made an error accept responsibility, to others if necessary and to yourself for sure. If you refuse to accept responsibility for a mistake you have made, you are choosing to play the blame game. Trying to place blame on someone drains energy from your quest and can set you back even further.

Another bad aspect of the blame game is the damage that it does to relationships. You may be able to browbeat someone into admitting that a mistake was their fault, but if it was really yours then you will both know it and the relationship may be damaged beyond repair. Once again, stay true to your values and take responsibility when it's yours to take.

The true success is one in which you maintain three positive attributes – accountability, responsibility and perseverance. These three traits are fantastic replacements for placing blame.

The amount of accountability, responsibility or perseverance that you can demonstrate at any given time will vary, depending on circumstances. Remember, you're a human being, not a robot. The good news is that you don't have to be perfect. Human frailty is something that even the greatest leaders, the most successful people in the world have to contend with. Somehow, despite their weaknesses, these leaders keep succeeding. If you find yourself in a bad moment, keep your chin up – you're in good company.

What exactly are these three miracle ingredients? *Accountability* is when you decide that you are the one who put yourself in your present situation. There are no excuses and no blame. When you're a true self leader, you quit giving yourself a built-in escape hatch.

In today's society there are too many people who want to blame others for their own poor decisions. Our current culture seems to cultivate a "victim mind set," where it's always someone else's fault regardless of how much we contributed to our own downfall. As a leader, you don't have this luxury.

Accountability means that you take the consequences for your actions. When it comes time to answer for a situation, you raise your hand. Not only do you cheat yourself when you let others take the blame for something you did, you also poison the relationships you have with other people. It takes moral courage to be accountable for your actions, a moral courage that most people rarely see. This is what enables you to achieve success.

Responsibility means that you make and keep promises, both to yourself and to others. Keeping promises and commitments is one of the most powerful tools that a successful person can implement. Again, our culture has made it acceptable – if not fashionable – for people to break promises.

You need only to read the newspaper to see examples of broken promises. Professional athletes want to "renegotiate" their contracts. Business executives are arrested for embezzling funds from their clients, shareholders or employees. Politicians are notorious for making promises during a campaign, then reneging on them after the election.

On a smaller but more common scale, think of the number of people who make appointments for which they arrive late, or even break. Look at deadlines for deliveries that were set, but missed. Some people are known for "always being late." These people show a lack of personal responsibility.

If you are going to be late, make it a point to call and let people know. It's very annoying when people don't stand up to their mistakes and try to make light of it in some indirect way. All these things add up to the way people perceive you.

Make it a point from this point on to keep your promises. If you're unsure about your ability to fulfill a commitment, then don't make the commitment. A good rule of business conduct is, "Under promise and over deliver."

In our culture we have become so jaded and inured to promises being broken that the person who keeps his word stands out.

As you keep promises to other people, you become the one that they know they can count on. That type of reputation is invaluable to a leader who wants to get things done. As you keep your promises, appointments and commitments to others, you will find that more and more they will keep their commitments to you. Not only are you demonstrating self leadership, you become an example and a leader to others.

Keeping promises to yourself is just as important as keeping promises to others and is a prerequisite to keeping promises to others. To achieve more, you have to develop success habits. You develop these habits by getting into daily routines that develop you in ways you may have ignored before. It may be to start exercising regularly, or to write in a daily journal. Whatever it is, you have to make a commitment to work on these areas at specific times on a steady basis, so that they become a habit. Remember, it takes about three weeks to create a new habit.

One psychological aspect of keeping promises to yourself is that you will discover that blaming others for problems ceases to be an option for you. Most of us are in the habit of putting promises to ourselves low on the list of priorities, when in reality there is nothing more important.

Results matter. Responsibility also means, to paraphrase a famous slogan, just doing it. Someone once said that ninety percent of success is simply showing up. Although simplistic, the idea behind it contains a kernel of real truth. Simply, as a minimum, doing the things that are expected of you is one way to be ahead of almost everyone else. Always strive for the best possible result, doing the best work of which you are capable. Taking care of business prevents logjams and delays further along your road to success.

Perseverance

Perseverance is sticking with your course of action regardless of how difficult it is. As I mentioned earlier, being a human being is tough. As hard as it is now, however, it's nothing compared to what the early settlers and pioneers had to go through.

Imagine if you had to travel across the continent in a wagon drawn by mules or oxen, suffering in freezing cold and debilitating heat. It puts having to wait on an elevator in perspective, doesn't it?

Of course, we have to contend with things that pioneers didn't have to worry about. The enormous number of social interactions we have to go through on a daily basis is staggering. We have to count on other people for so many of our needs, and each one of them is capable of disappointing us – broken promises, lies, backstabbing and other negative qualities are too often part of the equation when dealing with people. In the world of business, perseverance has you hold course. That is why having a clear vision and eye on the end-result is so important. When someone puts up a roadblock – you find a way around it.

Perseverance means accepting that there will be hardships and pressing on anyway. If you can't accomplish your task one way, find another. Most of what we consider problems are actually inconveniences. You have tremendous resources at your disposal if you only look for them. Demonstrating perseverance means that you don't let the closure of one avenue prevent you from achieving what you want or need to do.

One thing that perseverance does not mean is compromising your values. Sure, there are short cuts and easier ways to get some things done, but if you feel that you have to violate your ethics to accomplish a goal then you haven't looked hard enough. We face almost unbearable pressure to cut corners or cheat to get things done. Doing the right thing is always harder than cheating, but if you start down the road to unethical behavior, then you are violating a promise to yourself, the promise to align your actions with your values. As a result you will never reach long lasting and enduring success.

For the person who has tasted true success, who wants more in life, and who is determined to follow his or her passion and dream, perseverance will always remain a required trait. The nature of problems may change with circumstances, but never giving up will forever be the best strategy.

May you reach enduring success!

ABOUT THE AUTHOR

Oliver Pecora is a true entrepreneur. After building his business, he learned how to create balance in his own life. Today his passion lies in helping others reach for their own dreams, while showing them how to balance that vision with the bigger picture - living life.

Oliver's resolve to build a successful life for himself goes back to his early teens in Hayward, California, when he helped at his mother's Delicatessen and in his step-father's Tool & Die shop. Almost every summer he also found himself helping in his uncle's painting and design business in Frankfurt, Germany.

Oliver's advanced education includes completion of a Tool and Die Apprenticeship in Southern Germany in the late 1980's, and shortly thereafter, earning his Mechanical Engineering degree, also in Germany.

Later, Oliver co-founded his first business in Germany. He specialized in helping other companies comply with quality management standards, as well as leverage technology to meet those standards. It was at this time that much of his theoretical education helped him achieve practical success in day-to-day business. He also became more aware of the challenges companies face in meeting high quality standards that help them achieve the coveted ISO Certification.

Interested in a new start and seeking more creative freedom, Oliver moved back to California. In 1997 he founded his company, SIC Consulting. He currently resides in Northern California with his wife and two children.

Oliver enjoys aviation and is a licensed private pilot. Oliver has a natural curiosity for life, a sense of purpose, and a focused passion in all of his pursuits.

www.ingramcontent.com/pod-product-compliance
Lightning Source LLC
Chambersburg PA
CBHW021401090426
42742CB00009B/952

* 9 7 8 1 5 9 9 3 0 4 2 5 0 *